MIKE ROOT

SPILT GRAPE JUICE

RETHINKING THE WORSHIP TRADITION

 COLLEGE PRESS
PUBLISHING COMPANY
Joplin, Missouri

Library of Congress Catalog Card Number: 92-73572
International Standard Book Number: 0-89900-421-0

CONTENTS

SECTION FOUR
ENJOYMENT AND THE ASSEMBLY

SECTION FIVE
EVANGELISM AND THE ASSEMBLY

SUMMARY

PREFACE

The new young missionary to India, troubled about the malnourished poor Indians, couldn't understand why they were starving when so many cows were around. When he expressed his concern to the older and much wiser missionary, he was told, "Don't ask." Most Christians have wondered why "church" services are so traditional, so formally structured, and so irrelevant to contemporary times. But, when they expressed their concerns, the answer they have received is "Don't ask."

I knew before I wrote the first word of this book that I would be dealing with the biggest "sacred cow" in the church. But, I was – and am – firmly convinced that we are long overdue in asking some tough questions about an area that dominates our religious life. Christians should never be afraid to ask questions about what they do, especially when their questions involve something central to faith. The

7

assembly has the potential for being the most enriching, exciting and revitalizing time of the week, but unfortunately, many times our meeting together ends up being nothing more than the fulfillment of a religious requirement.

The intent of this study is to challenge the readers' thinking. I hoped the book will generate profitable discussions and some improvements in the assemblies. Some, who feel threatened by my conclusions, probably will write this book off as heretical and blasphemous and will probably merely be recommitted to their traditional thinking. Others, however, will read things that will make them say, "I've been thinking that for years. I'm glad to see someone else feels that way."

This book is not an exhaustive study of the assembly with loads of Greek and Hebrew and in-depth historical background. I have written it for "normal" people who like to read and aren't afraid to do some thinking for themselves. That is also why I have not emphasized "how to's" in this book. Applying the ideas and principles discussed in this study is the job of the individual Christian and the individual congregation. You don't need me to develop a new list of traditions.

I followed a formula that I use when I preach. I like to be simple, logical and biblical. I also like to be positive and upbeat. I was, however, somewhat negative in a few areas of this book to give the point emphasis and in order to express some of the frustration that most Christians occasionally feel about their assemblies. I hope you find this book thought provoking and helpful, but most of all, I hope you find it biblically accurate.

Give all the glory to God and all the criticism to me – *after* you've thoroughly thought it through.

Mike Root

SECTION ONE
EXAMINE THE ASSEMBLY

CHAPTER ONE
Tea and Thee

I always looked forward to our chorus trip to beautiful, sparkling, historic St. Augustine. The air was warm and filled with the smell of salt water and orange blossoms. Of all the trips our high-school chorus made each year, this trip was the one we enjoyed most.

The church hosting our trip spread a sumptuous potluck luncheon for us at the community center. It was one of those lazy, sunny Sunday afternoons when a nap was desired, but a walk would have to suffice. Several of us decided to tour one of the ornate cathedrals just down the street from the community center. With plastic cups of iced tea in hand, we strolled over to an entrance of the cathedral and stood awe-struck by the massive building with its mammoth spires and hand-carved mahogany doors.

We were joined by other visitors who hoped to get a guided tour of the spectacular piece of architecture. When the doors were opened, we were greeted by a stern faced elderly lady, who gestured for us to enter the building.

I don't know whether the coolness of the building was due to air conditioning or the marble floors and vaulted ceiling. The sight that met us was a cloistered collage of hardwood panels, statues in pale pastels, gold chandeliers, and brass candlesticks. The dramatic setting brought an instantaneous hush to the excited tourists.

Our gray-haired guide turned to face us and began what promised to be an informative dissertation on art, history and Catholicism. Suddenly she caught her breath and stared at me with horror-filled eyes.

"How dare you come into the house of God with food and drink?" she shrilled.

I was completely dumfounded. What in the world could she be talking about? Then my memory bank focused in on the cold cup sweating in my hand. Could that possibly be what she was uptight about? I held the cup up as if to say, "Is this the problem?"

"Yes," she answered, "I'm afraid I have to ask you to leave the building. We can't have that in here."

She said it so harshly that I was tempted to give her a smart-aleck response, such as "If I spill anything on God's floor, I'll clean it up," but I knew that wasn't the sort of thing a teenager from a Christian school should say.

We left the "hallowed ground" in shock and disappointment. In spite of the bright blue skies, I was sure I saw a black cloud hovering over that cathedral.

Now, it looked more like a castle for Count Dracula than a "house for God." Isn't it amazing how quickly one's perspective changes when one has been made to feel unwelcomed?

That incident happened over 20 years ago, and I still can feel the sadness I had in my heart. I was not sad because I'd been booted out of a cathedral, but sad because the matriarch of that cathedral had no idea where God really lived. God lives in people, not property. I find it disturbing to think how much has changed since the days of the New Testament church when Christians met "from house to house."

Not long ago, a middle-aged lady came to me to express her desire to place membership with our congregation. She had attended church faithfully all her life, but she had not gone anywhere during the last year. She skipped over the reason for her recent lack of attendance and went on to discuss how pleased she was with our services and my preaching (so it was a bad time for me to interrupt). As she prepared to leave my office, she stopped and said, "This is going to sound silly, but you know why I haven't been attending church? I had surgery on my foot, and the only shoes I could wear were tennis shoes. I just felt I couldn't come to church wearing tennis shoes. What would people think?"

Like the people on the day of Pentecost in Acts 2, I was "pierced to the heart." What have we done to New Testament worship that has caused it to become so twisted? *What have we done to the simplicity of Christians coming together in the name of love, unity and Christ?* We have preached fervently that the church building is not the church; the members are the church. We have lambasted the brethren for acting as if the assembly were a fashion show, and we have decried the false belief that going to church is all we need to do as Christians. Yet, we find ourselves unintentionally propagating all of these things because we have structured our religion around "going to church."

Every fledgling evangelist has hit his congregation with "Going to church doesn't make you a Christian any more than going into a henhouse makes you a chicken." Who has not used or at least seen the famous visual illustration where the preacher takes off his coat and puts it back on to symbolize people who take their Christianity off after church on Sunday only to put it on again in seven days. Sunday-morning Christians, pew sitters and churchgoers have been fuel for many fire-and-brimstone sermons.

When will our attitudes about meeting together change? Are preachers ineffective? Has God given us an impossible task? Did the New Testament Christians ever have this problem?

These questions scare me because as long as we continue to misunderstand the nature of the assembly our attitudes will never change; preachers will never be effective; and we will continue to have little in common with the assemblies of the New Testament church.

One thing most churches have in common, even when they are doctrinally opposed to one another, is an allegiance to assembling together. In fact, many have a religion of the assembly. The assembly has become the god to be worshiped and obeyed. Attendance is the criterion for judging faithfulness, and presence is synonymous with spiritual growth. *We have created a "get your ticket punched" approach to justification that fosters false security and promotes marginal involvement.* We preach that attendance is not everything, but then expect it will be the only thing we get.

In the Bible the assembly is never used as a whip to threaten other Christians. Attendance is never seen as a spiritual abacus to count members' devotion or pictured as the primary activity or most important event in a Christian's life. In fact, we have to do some fancy exegesis to justify our ardent belief in the pre-eminence of "going to church." We have demanded much more from Hebrews 10:25 than was ever intended by its writer and inspirer. A misunderstanding of the scripture is evidenced by a church bulletin I received in the mail once. Below the picture of the church building on the front page was a caption: VISITORS WELCOMED – MEMBERS EXPECTED.

Not long ago we had a special assembly of our church. Rather than have our normal two services and Bible class in the morning and an evening service that night, we had a combined and longer assembly, after which we had a dinner-on-the-grounds. Then we closed out with an old-fashioned singing service and devotional. We met together from 10:30 a.m. to 2:30 p.m. and went home for the rest of the day.

That evening, as I sat down to watch *60 Minutes* for the first time in my life, a strange cloud of guilt settled over my head. The guilt came not because I was watching *60 Minutes*, but because I was not "at church." I knew better, but old ideas die slowly.

With this study I do not intend to re-invent the wheel. My intent is for us to see the wheel as a part of a moving structure and not the structure itself. We need to see the assembly as a tool and not the total, a

15

means and not an end, a catalyst and not catatonic. To accomplish this goal we must go the New Testament and rediscover the nature of the assembly.

DISCUSSION QUESTIONS

1. How central is the assembly to your personal religious life?

2. What does it mean to have a "religion of the assembly"?

3. Is the assembly the high point of your week? Why or why not?

4. What is the primary purpose of the assembly?

5. If you have a Sunday morning and evening assembly, which one is the most important? Why? Do all the other members of your congregation agree with you?

CHAPTER TWO
Pardon My Myth

We are the product of nearly 20 centuries of churchgoing. Our roots are firmly cemented in the beliefs that the church building is sacred and the worship service is the most important event of the week. These beliefs began with the advent of Catholicism, and the Reformation did little to alter it for Protestants. We have been raised to believe that Sunday is holy, and some states still have "blue laws" on the books to enforce it. Few words have more cultural significance than "church," "Sunday," and "worship." These words are so steeped in tradition and wrapped by our emotions that going back to the Bible becomes an extremely touchy proposition. At the very least, we find it difficult to examine the subject with an open mind.

Every history professor repeatedly warns his students about the dangers of "present mindedness." Present mindedness is the disastrous habit we have of examining history by modern standards and with contemporary prejudices. Hindsight is not even perfect when looking at the recent past, but when we look at the ancient past we tend to have severely slanted vision. Such altered vision is especially dangerous when we go to the Bible to find support for what we already believe instead of looking for new insights.

One of the challenges inherent in "handling accurately the word of truth" (2 Timothy 2:15) is the need to be open and receptive to that truth. We must try to view New Testament concepts through first century eyes whenever we can, especially if we are concerned with following the example set by those early Christians.

Try to peruse the New Testament as if your eyes had never seen a "church building" or Sunday marked on a calendar and as if your ears never had heard a sermon about church attendance. Thinking this way you begin to see a whole new church unfold. In this church outward appearances are de-emphasized and the assembly is not a requirement but a blessing too good to miss. For New Testament Christians, the assembly was a time when Christians got together to be together and not because they had to perform, conform or dodge guilt. In gathering for worship the dominant concern was walking "with all humility and gentleness, with patience, showing forbearance to one another in love, being diligent to preserve the unity of the Spirit in the bond of peace"

18

(Ephesians 4:2,3).

Christians in the New Testament were not perfect. From Ananias and Sapphira in Acts 5 to the seven churches of Asia in Revelation, the early saints had problems, not the least of which was 2,000 years of Jewish traditions that had to be overcome. Does that sound familiar?

In the New Testament we see people who fell into the same traps we do today. They had folks who keyed in on law and not love and who preached a spirit of uniformity rather than the Spirit of Christ. The Jewish Christians in Jerusalem insisted on circumcision and obedience to the law of Moses (Acts 15:5), and the false apostles in Corinth were making slaves of their brethren and slapping them around as if they were punching bags (2 Corinthians 11:13, 20). In Rome, Christians ostracized members who had opinions different from theirs (Romans 14). In every case problems arose because believers had forgotten that Christ brought freedom and not an exchange of prisons.

Nowhere is this tendency seen more clearly today than in the burdensome, legalistic and often times counterproductive approach many take toward the assembly. Few things get people in an uproar faster than challenging their beliefs about the assembly. Brethren leave congregations over whether the Lord's Supper should be served before or after the sermon. If you change the time of the assembly, you risk changing the make-up of your church. Probably no issue has split more churches than the cost, design and location of a new building, all of which are totally in the realm of expediency. These types of problems will always exist when "going to church" is the most important

19

part of one's religion.

Before we explore the nature of the assembly in the New Testament, let's examine what it was not. To emphasize these as negatives, I will refer to them as myths about the assembly.

MYTH #1: *The New Testament church met in order to worship.* Before you drop this book to run and purchase some tar and feathers, let me clarify the statement. All my life, going to worship was synonymous with going to church. On many occasions I entered an auditorium that had a sign over the door. The sign read, "Enter to Worship – Leave to Serve." That statement is both right and wrong. The idea is right because we do worship inside, but the idea is wrong because we never enter or leave worship.

We will have Sunday-only Christians as long as we have Sunday-only worship. *We have been fighting a losing battle because we have been proclaiming that Christianity is something "you are," but worship is something "you do." Nothing could be farther from the truth. If you are a Christian you are worship to God.* The matter is not one of *doing* but rather of *being.*

We need to define worship, which should not be obscured in theological jargon. Worship is as simple as the gospel itself. Worship is a life given in obedience to Christ. At one time worship was the act of going to the temple and making a sacrifice, but in Christ, we sacrifice ourselves. Our lives become worship to God. Let's paint a portrait of worship using the Word of God.

I urge you therefore, brethren, by the mercies of God, to present your bodies a living and holy sacrifice, acceptable to God, which is your spiritual service of worship. And do not be conformed to this world, but be transformed by the renewing of your mind, that you may prove what the will of God is, that which is good and acceptable and perfect. (Romans 12:1,2)

Therefore, since we receive a kingdom which cannot be shaken, let us show gratitude, by which we may offer to God an acceptable service with reverence and awe; for our God is a consuming fire. (Hebrews 12:28,29)

Through Him then, let us continually offer up a sacrifice of praise to God, that is, the fruit of lips that give thanks to His name. And do not neglect doing good and sharing; for with such sacrifices God is pleased. (Hebrews 13:15,16)

Whether, then, you eat or drink or whatever you do, do all to the glory of God. (1 Corinthians 10:31)

And whatever you do in word or deed, do all in the name of the Lord Jesus. (Colossians 3:17)

While these passages have many things in common, the one thread that weaves its way through them all is the completeness of being a child of God. Sacrifice, worship, service, glorifying God and representing Jesus are all a way of life. You don't "go to it" any more than a fish goes for a swim. Worship is what you are - a worshipping creature and a sacrifice to God that is complete and continual.

In these passages, many things that are usually thought of as acts are described here as being life-enveloping. At one time, God's people offered sacrifices at all the appropriate occasions. Now, we are a "living sacrifice," and as such are constantly worshiping God. Now we give God "acceptable service with reverence" instead of being reverent on special occasions or in sacred places. We don't have to go anywhere to praise God because we "continually offer up

21

a sacrifice of praise to God." As Christians, we do everything "to the glory of God" and "in the name of Jesus." Our lives are not segmented or spiritually compartmentalized because we have given ourselves completely to Him.

WHOLLY WORSHIP

Two primary words in the New Testament are translated into worship. These words are *proskuneo* and *latreuo*.

Thayer defines *proskuneo* as "to prostrate one's self hence in the New Testament by kneeling or prostrating to do homage or make obeisance." Arndt and Gingrich add that it is "the custom of prostrating oneself before a person and kissing his feet, the garment, the ground, etc." [2] *Proskuneo* is the word used by Jesus in John 4:20-24 as He described to the woman at the well what God wanted from worshippers. This word also was used concerning a slave before his master (Matthew 18:26) and by Satan who wanted Jesus to "fall down and worship" him (Matthew 4:9).

With the exception of John before the angel in Revelation, we find no place where New Testament Christians prostrated themselves and paid homage. They kissed each other (Romans 16:16); they gave thanks in all circumstances (1 Thessalonians 5:18); they prayed without ceasing (v. 17). But they never went anywhere for the express purpose of doing obeisance. They led lives of obedience. *Proskuneo* was what they were, not what they did.

Latreuo is defined as "to serve, minister to; in the New Testament to render religious service or homage,

22

to worship."[3] *Latreuo* is the word used in Romans 12:1 to describe what our "living sacrifice" is. The word is both worship and service. Worship and service are interchangeable. This concept is the key to understanding what New Testament worship is all about. Both are nutshell descriptions of what the Christian life is. We have given ourselves to God as living sacrifices and He has declared our lives to be worship to Him. Every day we place our lives on the altar and sacrifice ourselves to His service.

Robert Cushman, in his classic article on "Worship as Acknowledgment," gave us a beautiful definition of worship. He said, "Worship is simply life that, in entire truthfulness, is given back into the hands of Him who gave it."[4] William Barclay echoed the same sentiments when he called on Christians to "Take your body; take all the tasks you have to do everyday; take the ordinary work of the shop, the factory, the shipyard, the mine; and offer all that as an act of worship to God."[5]

We have done a terrible disservice to worship when we confine it to a passive, localized and selective gathering and time. Worship is a "living sacrifices" and that life is constant. With every beat of a heart that is living for God, He is glorified and worshiped. In connection with Romans 12:1, V.L. Stanfield concluded, "Worship and service are inseparably united. In response to what God has done for him in Christ, man surrenders himself completely to God."[6]

As I write this chapter, I can see the rebirth of spring outside my window. Grass is gradually transforming from brown to green, as God intended. Trees are sprouting buds, as God intended. Birds of every shape and color are fluttering around after having

23

spent the winter in a warmer climate, again, as God intended. All these things are part of nature's way of praising God. They are all doing the things God intended for them to do.

When you and I do the things God intended for us to do, we are living "to the praise of his glory" (Ephesians 1:14). To put it another way, we are worshiping Him. Paul stressed this principle throughout the first chapter of his letter to the Ephesians. God called us to live a life of praise to Him. This happens when we receive His grace, (v. 6), when we hope in Christ (v. 12) and when we listen to His message and believe His promises (v. 13,14). Praising God is worshiping God, and Paul has declared that praise is a way of life for Christians.

Several years ago, a fellow minister and I watched a cat catch a small green lizard. We watched in horror as the orange feline fed on its prey. The lizard was not gobbled up, but was eaten slowly, one bite at a time, starting with its tail. From a human standpoint the method seemed cruel and criminal. From nature's perspective the cat was simply being a cat. It didn't know how to be anything else. The cat was being what God intended for it to be.

Worship is our attempt to be all that God wants us to be. It "is the submission of all our nature to God . . . the surrender of our will to His purpose."[7]

One of the best definitions of worship was given by one of the most popular writers of our time, Warren Wiersbe. In his short but inspiring book *Real Worship,* he used this working definition:

> Worship is the believer's response of all that he is-mind, emotions, will, and body-to all that God is and says and does. This response has its mystical side in subjective experience, and its practical side in objective obedience to God's revealed truth. It is a loving response that is balanced by the fear of the Lord, and it is a deepening response as the believer comes to know God better.[8]

When we read passages in the New Testament that refer to Christians assembling together, we impose our erroneous viewpoint and say, "See, they're coming together to worship!" That statement is true if you mean it as an extension of their living worship, but it is false if you mean they were meeting to do something that only happened when they were together. In the New Testament they never mentioned "going to worship," "having a worship service," or performing "acts of worship." They would not know what we are talking about because they were "offering uninterrupted worship."[9]

When we think of worship, we should think of living for God and not have mental pictures of build- ✗ point *ings, reverent atmospheres, long faces and structured acts. Worship is synonymous with sacrifice, praise, obedience and service.* Worship is the person we help who has been left for dead by the roadside, and not just the three hours at "church" on Sunday. Worship is the cup of cold water given on Tuesday as well as the cup of grape juice taken on the first day of the week. Worship comes from a heart that houses God and not just from what tradition calls "the house of God." But then, that's getting into another myth.

25

DISCUSSION QUESTIONS

1. What are some of the things that must never be done in your church building? Why?

2. What are some of the dangers involved in "present mindedness"?

3. What is the traditional definition of worship?

4. Does coming to understand that worship is a way of life as opposed to a block of time on Sunday change a person? If so, how?

5. How and when does a Christian praise God?

CHAPTER THREE
We Sure Mythed That One

MYTH #2: The New Testament church met to establish traditions. Any preacher worth his salt will tell you his primary task is to preach the message of Christ. We preachers love to fume and flail and proclaim to any critic that we preach "Christ and Him crucified." We "speak as it were the oracles of God"; we "preach the Word"; we are "instant in season and out of season." How is it then, that we are either hesitant or apologetic when we have to attack some church tradition? "Well, that's not preaching Christ," declares some sincere Christian.

Is there a difference in preaching Christ and preaching the message of Christ? I think not. Did Jesus have anything to say about traditions? If you've read the

Gospels lately, you know He had a great deal to say about traditions.

The Jews – Pharisees in particular – had reached a point in their religious history where they couldn't tell the difference between what was God's law and what was man's tradition. Jesus never attacked their allegiance to the law of Moses, but He condemned their insistence on binding traditions. Virtually every conflict He had with them was about traditions.

Important point

God's law vs man's tradition

A righteous smile must have been on the faces of the Pharisees and scribes when they questioned Jesus about His disciples and their unclean habits. Not only were the disciples guilty of violating tradition, but they were not purifying or cleansing themselves before eating. Seeking external criteria for judging others is typical for the religious.

The response Jesus gave to the Pharisees in Matthew 15:3-9 is applicable to tradition worshippers of any age. He said that because of their traditions they did three things: They transgressed the commands of God (v. 3), invalidated the word of God (v. 6), worshiped in vain (v. 9).

Traditions may be beneficial for social cohesion, but if they are exalted to a position of law, they always will cause people to disobey God, be insensitive to His Word, and make their worship unacceptable to Him. Few things in the Gospel are given more attention by Jesus than traditions. We have a divine obligation to warn God's people of the danger of emphasizing traditions. If we are truly going to be loyal to Jesus' message, we must present it the way He did, even if it's not the traditional thing to do.

Paul said,

See to it that no one takes you captive through philosophy and empty deception, according to the tradition of men, according the elementary principles of the world, rather than according to Christ. (Colossians 2:8)

The New Testament church waged a constant battle to keep the customs of the Jews from being required of all Christians. Had they cast off the yoke of law and tradition only to create some new ones? We need to be reminded that the first-century church had no one to copy. They had Judaism, but that was not to be copied. They did not need traditions to reinforce unity. Their unity was in Christ. He was the One they sought to copy and not some man-made customs.

So, who decided what church buildings were supposed to look like? Who came up with a pew? Why do we meet Sunday morning and not Sunday afternoon? Why is the assembly one hour long? Why do we dress up to be with family? Who came up with the order of service? Why do we call it a worship service? The list is much longer, and the answer is the same for each question: tradition.

In the book of Acts there is a noticeable absence of instructions for Christians to build, establish and maintain traditions. The church was not built on traditions, and the assembly was not to foster traditions. Christians came together for a far more important and heartfelt reason.

However, the lack of stress on traditions is not to say that traditions should be anathema in the church. All of us have very warm memories of family traditions that we cherish dearly. Every school in the world has its own set of traditions which alumni talk about the rest of their lives. Congregations also have "church traditions" that are very important to the ongoing heritage of its people. Things like giving out Bibles to new Christians, roasting hot dogs on the Fourth of July, or having a Rook tournament on New Year's Eve can be important bonding elements for a congregation. The danger is in elevating any tradition to a position of spiritual orthodoxy and unbreakable, unchangeable law.

MYTH #3: The New Testament church met to perform rituals. Many see worship in the Bible as a natural progression of meeting places. We conclude that worship went from the altar, to the tabernacle, to the temple, to the church building. We see it including ritualistic activities like sacrifice, prayer and cleansing. Yet, at the same time, God's people always have missed the most important element in the entire scheme of things.

Hosea wrote, "For I delight in loyalty rather than sacrifice, and in the knowledge of God rather than burnt offering" (6:6). Earlier, Samuel had to be reminded that God is not interested in externals but in the heart. He said, "For God sees not as man sees, for man looks at the outward appearance, but the Lord looks at the heart" (1 Samuel 16:7).

No theme is more consistent in the Bible than the call for mankind to "love the Lord your God with all your heart" (Deuteronomy 13:3; Matthew 22:37). This theme reverberates throughout the sacred pages, reminding us that He is the true object of our worship and that worship must take place in our hearts. Just as surely as God sees hearts and not houses, He sees righ-

30

teousness and not rituals.

In the New Testament, Christians are told that God judges hearts (Matthew 5:28; 12:34,35; 15:18,19; Hebrews 4:12), that we are His temple (1 Corinthians 6:19), that and we are "a sacrifice of praise to God" (Hebrews 13:15). What do all these biblical truths have in common? They all emphasize the preeminent position of the heart as the meeting place between God and man. We obey from the heart (Romans 6:17); we believe in our heart (Romans 10:9); and we draw near with a true heart (Hebrews 10:22).

So what is the big deal? The big deal is the tendency we have of ritualizing and thereby trivializing matters of the heart. *Our religion has become a performance or a series of acts that have become the object of our worship instead of pointing us to the object of our worship.* We have devised a system that emphasizes motion and not motives. "We are just trying to follow the Bible," someone declares. This statement is not true if you have made a ritual out of something God meant to be an act of love and if "doing all the right things" is more important than having the right kind of heart.

One of the most convicting examples of this is found in the Sermon on the Mount. Jesus, speaking to a Jewish audience, described a scenario where a Jew was going to the temple to offer a sacrifice, which was one of the most important "acts" in the life of any Jew. If while presenting that offering, he remembered that a brother was at odds with him, Jesus said that he was to drop everything and go straighten out the problem with his brother (Matthew 5:23,24). Why? God wants consistency in our faith, and consistency is only possible when our faith is from our hearts.

31

The primary message of Matthew 6 is that we should do no religious act to be seen by people. Prayer, fasting and giving are matters of the heart, and "your Father who sees in secret will repay you." Is it not odd that we put so much emphasis on being seen of other persons at the right time and place?

"To be converted to faith in Jesus Christ is to return to the worship of the true God," says Graham Kendrick, "and to dethrone all rivals to his authority. The very heart of worship is the giving, not only of our talents and goods, but of our selves."[10] A ritual can be a rival if it becomes the thing worshiped. If you "go to worship," then it has to be a thing or a place. It also becomes something you go from.

Gene Getz says we suffer from "creeping institutionalism." This happens when "dogmas and traditions and its forms and structures" become "more important than the people themselves." Rather than helping each other develop a deeper, more personal relationship with God, the church has become no different than "a club, society, or group in the secular world. In many cases traditions overshadowed the Word of God." Too much emphasis is placed on conforming to the group standards and almost no emphasis given to daily spiritual growth. "People religiously performed routines and rituals, but without true spiritual meaning. Their religion became a matter of form and ceremony, not life and experience. A personal relationship with an organization."[11]

"All right kids," said the excited father, "here's the plan. We need to get an early start on our trip to the lake. So, we'll sit in the back of the church building. As soon as communion is over and before the sermon starts, we'll ease out the back door." Thus a great symbol of love and sacrifice is demoted from *koinonia* to a ticket-punched ritual.

"Our heavenly Father," booms the mellifluous voice of the good brother leading the official prayer. Heads bow, eyes close, and minds wander. Not everyone's of course, but who hasn't been surprised by an unexpected "Amen" that signals it's time to come in from left field? We've gone through the motions, but our hearts have stayed in neutral.

The point of the chapter is not to be judgmental but to recognize that when we view worship in terms of rituals, we will inevitably develop a form religion that is powerless (2 Timothy 3:5). We need to remember the Words of God as He spoke through the prophet Amos:

> I hate, I reject your festivals, nor do I delight in your solemn assemblies. Even though you offer up to Me burnt offerings and your grain offerings, I will not accept them; and I will not even look at the peace offerings of your fatlings. Take away from Me the noise of your songs; I will not even listen to the sound of your harps. But let justice roll down like water and righteousness like an ever-flowing stream. (5:21-24)

point

God is not sitting up in heaven on a gray marble throne, tabulating church attendance and checking off performed rituals. He gave His Son to be Lord of our hearts, not the accountant of our good works.

One of the reasons why many have failed to understand what appears to be God's selective enforcement of disobedience can be traced to our failure to grasp this principle. Were Nadab and Abihu the only ones who ever disobeyed God's ordinances (Numbers 3:4)? Why was poor Uzzah struck dead? Wasn't he just trying to be helpful? God's action caused David to be angry with Him (2 Samuel 6:6-8). Why were Ananias and Sapphira not given another chance (Acts 5:1-10)? We forget that in each of these cases God knew what we can't know - the condition of their hearts. If we see these only as acts of rebellion, we will quickly run into the problem of inconsistency.

In the New Testament we are called to be worshiping children. That worship is as much a part of our family life as breathing. Worship is an integral part of our relationship with our Father and our brothers and sisters. "Worship is to the Christian what the mainspring is to a watch, what the engine is to a car. It is the very core, the most essential element," said John MacArthur Jr. in his book, *The Ultimate Priority*. "Worship cannot be isolated or relegated to just one place, time, or segment of our lives."[12] MacArthur went on to give one of the best descriptions of worship I have read:

> Worship as the Word of God presents it is internal, sacrificial, active, and productive. That is not at all like the world's concept of worship, yet it is the only kind of worship God recognizes. It is the purest kind of worship - the kind that ascends to God as sweet incense, the kind that is expressed continuously in every aspect of our lives by sharing with others, doing good works, and offering praise to God. That is the kind of worship God desires. It is worship in its deepest, most spiritual sense.[13]

DISCUSSION QUESTIONS

1. What are some of the things that Jesus had to say about human traditions?

2. What are some of the traditions in your assemblies? Where did they come from, and how do they help your "togetherness"?

3. What is the danger in letting a congregational activity or a biblical command become a ritual?

4. What is the most important part of your assembly? Why?

5. How do you prevent an assembly activity, (such as prayer or the Lord's Supper) from being a "ticket-punched ritual"?

CHAPTER FOUR
Together All By Myself

While sitting in the Dallas-Fort Worth Airport some time ago, I decided to use my layover time wisely by working on a sermon for the next Sunday. As I sat there watching and thinking, a heart-rending analogy came to my mind, causing me to write a sermon about "The Church of the Airport."

The airport was filled with people who had many things in common.

1. We all shared a common belief – flying was the best way to travel.

2. We shared a common goal – arriving at a destination.

3. We shared a common facility – the airport.

4. We were all alone in the airport.

The Church of the Airport was complete with rituals, traditions, doctrine, goals and a building. Sadly enough, this church has about the same level of relationship building as many congregations. How many people are part of a group that calls itself a church and have much in common, yet are alone in the church building? If this is happening with any group claiming to follow the New Testament, they have not only missed the boat, they have missed the ocean it sails on.

Being alone in the church will always result when people assemble to reinforce traditions, worship rituals, and fulfill legal requirements. *The New Testament describes a living, powerful and turned-on faith, but we seem intent on maintaining a funeral parlor, sanctuary, formless pall over our assemblies and then wonder why our people have furrowed brows and sound like snakes saying "Shhhh."* Sometimes the only "joyful noise" heard in many assemblies is the final "Amen."

That statement was said not to be unkind, but rather to point out how completely different our assemblies are from what the New Testament churches were. Our assemblies resemble the Jewish temple worship more than the informal people oriented house assemblies of the early Christians. Apparently, Catholicism has been a far greater influence in causing Protestant churches to adopt a formal ritualistic approach to the assembly than the New Testament has in leading us to informal, yet meaningful assemblies. That may be a bold assumption on my part, but when I see formal ritualistic assemblies in place back through the Restoration and Reformation Movements to early Catholicism, but not in the New Testament times, it is the only conclusion I can reach.

As I said in Chapter 1, we are going to the Bible to find justification for what we are already doing, not to discover what we should be doing. This practice has caused us to miss or ignore the real reason why the New Testament Christians assembled.

SIMPLE RESEARCH

Before I address the real reason why they assembled, you may want to get a sheet of paper and list all the passages in the New Testament that deal with the assembly. It doesn't have to be a big sheet of paper. A small note pad will do. If you have a good concordance it won't take you but a couple of minutes.

Now that you've done that, what did you learn?

1. They met often and regularly.

2. They did several things when they met.

3. Very little is said in the New Testament about their assemblies.

In the face of this awesome silence, how is it that we have come to center our entire religion around the assembly and to feel so sure that we are doing it the way God wants it done? Much of the character of our assemblies comes from sources other than the Bible. The solemnity, the mysteriousness, the formality, the passivity, the performance, the traditions and the facilities, to mention just a few, do not have their roots in the 27 books of the New Testament. They can be found in Judaism, Catholicism, and in early American Puritanism, all of which have had a tremendous influence on all other Protestant churches in America.

It is sad to see well-meaning people twist the Scriptures to give credence to their beliefs about the assembly. When Jesus talked about worshiping God "in Spirit and in truth," was He calling for formalism? Heartfelt intensity, yes, but formalism? Was Paul's response to the chaotic assembly of the Corinthians a command to put on a long face and come to the assembly in mourning? Does "let all things be done properly and in an orderly manner" (1 Corinthians 14:40) mean that we are to solemnize and ritualize our activities? Or did Paul simply want Christians to maximize exhortation and minimize confusion (v. 31-33)?

In simple terms, we have emphasized the "what" of assemblies and missed the "why" of New Testament assemblies. We quickly go from the fact that they met to what they did when they met. The "whats" – sing, pray, partake of Lord's Supper, preach, and give – have become the objects of our assembly when the "why" should be the real object.

So, why did they meet? They met to be together.

Together is the one thing you can't do alone. They, the New Testament church, did not meet to fulfill requirements. They did not meet to pay back God. They did not meet just because it was expected. They did not meet out of a need to get some list of sacramental acts checked off. They met because they wanted to be together and because God wants His children to be together. This is the one common denominator shared by every New Testament passage on the assembly. With all their faults and growing pains, the early Christians were people who were together.

This idea may sound too simplistic to some and to others it may sound like blasphemy. Remember, the Christians in the New Testament didn't have to assemble in order to worship; they were worshiping with their lives. They were together because there were some things they could get only from being together, and there were some things that God wanted them to do together to enhance their togetherness and cause spiritual growth.

From the beginning "all those who had believed were together" (Acts 2:44). The "whole church" came together in Corinth to share and edify one another (1 Corinthians 14:23-26). They were together daily, from house to house, in the temple, in the market, and even in chains. They were not punching a clock or checking a list. They were together because one day they all would be taken up together to be with Jesus (1 Thessalonians 4:17).

"We don't assemble to be together," objects the Bible student. "We assemble to partake of the Lord's supper!" Clearly, that is a reason to assemble on the first day of the week. But, is it an act, a sacrament, or a togetherness builder? The very essence of the Lord's Supper is communion, *koinonia* or fellowship. As a memorial feast, it reinforces our commitment to a crucified Lord, but it also encourages, edifies and unites. It should be the most "together" thing we do. Anything less would make it a ritual.

Because of our emphasis on rituals or acts, we not only have robbed our assemblies of togetherness, but we have stripped them down to the bare minimum of required times. Attend one assembly a week, and you are faithful. Attend two a week, and you are a staunch supporter. Attend three a week, and you are a pillar of faith, destined to be given a title or at least an extra star in your crown.

The early church was a together church. As Everett

Ferguson discovered in his research of early writings,

> The encouragements to meet together in one place show the recognition by early Christians of the social dimension of their faith and the need frequently to be together. It is impossible to determine how many of these statements apply to the Lord's day assembly, but most seem to have in mind other assemblies as well.[14]

We grow when we are together because faith is contagious. Love, caring and godliness also are contagious. Unfortunately, if you want those things you have to find them in the foyer because once in the auditorium we have more important things to do. Have we forgotten that Jesus said the world recognizes us as His disciples because we love one another? That recognition does not come because we do all the right things on Sunday morning. We will talk about this in a later chapter, but there isn't much "one another" taking place in our assemblies.

Somehow, through the years, togetherness has been seen as an inferior reason for assembling. In spite of the clear emphasis in the New Testament on fellowship, oneness and unity, many have accepted the idea that we assemble to perform certain acts. Rather than seeing these acts as enhancements to togetherness, we have made them separate from and superior to togetherness. Relationship building and closeness are extra-curricular elements of the assembly. Many openly believe that "we don't come together to make friends, but to worship God," as if one somehow excludes the other.

Why is closeness reserved for the few minutes before and after the formal assembly or for those who participate in some informal get-together? "That's simple to answer," offers the bright young student, "You can't maintain the proper spirit of reverence when the setting is informal."

Formalism is in another chapter, so let's just look at what the Bible has to say about reverence in the New Testament assembly. I believe the word is zilch! Where did we get the idea? We either have imposed our "present mindedness" on to the New Testament, applied Old Testament concepts to the New Testament, or still yet, we have severely exhausted the limits of interpreting 1 Corinthians 14:40: "Let all things be done properly and in an orderly manner." *We insist on maintaining a structured and solemn assembly that not only is not found in the New Testament, but contributes to the army of those who are alone in the church.*

This is one of the searing questions asked by Jerry and Mary White in their book, *Friends and Friendship*.

> The church is the body of Christ – the fellowship of believers. It is the place where intimate friendships should spawn and grow. Yet is a place that often houses strangers – or so it seems to many who enter expecting a different world than the office, factory, or neighborhood. Many people do not find the friendships they seek and need in the church. The church should be one of the key seedbeds for deep friendships. What hinders the local church from functioning as an ideal catalyst to friendship?[15]

Rather than being a "catalyst to friendship," the assembly fosters a spirit of quiet, personal introspection and, in the name of reverential worship, is practically anti-relationship building. *There is a breakdown of togetherness in the church, which is due, at least partly, to the development of formalism in our assemblies.*

DISCUSSION QUESTIONS

1. Have you ever been in an assembly of Christians and felt all alone? When? How did you feel about it?

2. Describe a New Testament assembly. Explain why you believe it would be the way you describe it.

3. What is different about a 20th century assembly and a first century assembly?

4. Are fellowship and the assembly separate activities? Why?

5. Examine Acts 2:42-47, and see if you can determine where togetherness fit in their list of priorities.

CHAPTER FIVE
Keep Your Pinkie In The Air, Please

The one element that contributes considerably to the misunderstanding of worship, the sanctuary mentality, and the ritualizing of acts is formalism in the assembly. From where did "formalism" come? We refer to our assemblies as formal and informal, and we arbitrarily assign some things to each category based on traditional appropriateness, not on scripture.

How many times have you heard something described as "out of place in the formal assembly"? How many times have special presentations had to wait until after the official closing prayer? We act as though worship is something that can be turned on and off like a tape recorder.

Sunday morning is more formal than Sunday

evening; Sunday evening is more formal than Wednesday night Bible study; and Wednesday night is more formal than a devotional or retreat. Why? Who made that decision?

Formalism has its ironies. We dress up like butlers and then go to church to be served. We put on our long faces and funeral attitudes and tell each other we live for a risen Lord. Then we shake hands, admire attire, and call it togetherness. We've replaced spirituality with solemnity and changed unity to uniformity. Clearly we haven't restored New Testament Christianity; we have merely modified pre-Reformation traditions.

Such a pronouncement may sound harsh, but when you can't find a practice in the Bible, but you can find it in religious history, a red flag should be raised. Why haven't we seen that red flag?

For years people have been wondering why assemblies seem cold, boring, and in a rut. Man has made it that way, not God. He intended for His children to get together to strengthen each other, not to see how much they can endure.

Is formalism a man-made element of the assembly? Let's ask four questions that will help give us an answer.

First, where is the command, example or implied inference in the New Testament to justify formalism in the assembly?

Traditionally, we have used 1 Corinthians 14:40 as authorization for formalism. Paul said, "Let all things be done properly and in an orderly manner." Why did he say that? Evidently, the brethren in Corinth misunderstood the nature of the assembly. To them, the assembly was a showcase for spiritual gifts, a chance

46

to take center stage and impress everyone with their particular talent. They were being selfish and inconsiderate. As a result, visitors were confused and no one was being edified. The assembly had become chaotic. They had made a "one another" event an I'm-the-one event.

In 1 Corinthians 12, Paul tells those selfish individuals to think of the body. In Chapter 13, he tells them to desire love over spiritual gifts. And, in Chapter 14, he simply says, "Grow up." He closes the section by giving them three guiding principles for their assemblies. Make them peaceful (v. 33), do things properly, and do them in an orderly fashion (v 40). These principles give us a great deal of leeway. They are the same principles that govern most baseball games and 4-H Club meetings. The ideas certainly are not a prescription for formalism. They are simply basic Christian attitudes.

Other passages in the New Testament deal directly with our attitude, but really have no bearing on formalism. We must worship God in "spirit and truth" (John 4:24) and in a worthy manner (1 Corinthians 11:27), but these are matters of the heart, not ceremony. We must never allow anything to destroy these aspects of our assembly, even if it's something as innocent as a routine.

If you stay only in the New Testament, which is our covenant, not the Old Testament, and if you keep passages in context, you will discover no commands, examples or implied inferences that call on us to have formalism in our assemblies.

So where did formalism come from? One answer is that is came from man's tendency to emphasize externals. Keeping religion in the heart is too secretive and

*What did worship in
tabernacle call for?
Have we carried this over
to our assemblies?*

SPILT GRAPE JUICE

too difficult to judge. Mankind likes to have acts of
faith and a focal point from which to direct it. The
result is legalism and temple worship.

Clearly a degree of formalism was expected in the
Old Testament. The people in that era had both a legal
code to follow and an edifice to centralize their obedience. The tabernacle and the temple were the center
of individual and corporate religion. In the New Testament, the individual became the "temple of the Holy
Spirit": (1 Corinthians 6:19) and the priest; Jesus
became the High Priest. Church leadership and
brethren are support systems for the child of God, not
intermediaries.

In discussing these thoughts about formalism with
other students of the Bible, I have noticed a tendency
for them to immediately bring forth passages from the
Old Testament to use in defense of the traditional
thinking about the assembly. Passages are presented
from Psalms, Proverbs, and many of the prophets. We
should study these wonderful passages to instruct us
about the Old Covenant (1 Corinthians 10:11), to
encourage us (Romans 15:4), and to lead us to Christ
(Galatians 3:24), but not to give us insights into how
the New Testament church assembled.

Studying the Old Testament will help us to learn
more about the nature and attributes of God, which
are unchangeable, but in the New Covenant, we don't
respond to Him with a fatted calf; we offer ourselves
as a living sacrifice. The fact that people have to go to
the Old Testament to find supportive passages simply
shows how strongly some want to cling to traditional
ways. What other New Testament doctrines do we
substantiate with Old Testament proof texts?

We always need to study and know prophecy and

fulfillment. We need to clearly understand the unfolding plan of God to redeem man. But, we have no more a right to bind the formalism of tabernacle and temple worship than we do to bind circumcision. Our interest is directed toward "faith working through love" (Galatians 5:6), which is the heart of the New Covenant.

We stress that the church is people not buildings; then we sing "The Lord is in His holy temple, let all the earth keep silent before Him" to remind folks they're in a holy place. Church auditoriums are places you whisper, dress up, and don't dare carry a cup of coffee into. Listen sometime to the reasons given to small children about why they shouldn't run in the auditorium after the assembly.

For several hundred years the church met in homes, outdoors, and at other informal places. As Everett Ferguson points out, "Not until the age of Constantine do we find specially constructed buildings. Any space where an assembly was permitted was a possible site for a Christian gathering."[16]

It stands to reason that when you have a formal place for the assembly, you will have formal assemblies. Yet it doesn't have to be that way. The Bible doesn't teach it, but tradition demands it.

Secondly, what criterion is used to determine when an assembly is formal or informal?

In my experience, people always have understood that a Bible class is less formal than a Sunday morning assembly. Everyone assumes a retreat or small group devotional is informal and not under the same restrictions as a formal assembly. Therefore, in these settings, having dialogue, sharing ideas, and being flexible with the format are acceptable practices.

When we go to the Bible to find what guidelines we should use to determine which assemblies are formal and which are informal, we are stopped by silence.

Is size a determining factor? I have taught Bible classes of hundreds and preached to Sunday morning assemblies of three. Which was formal? In the New Testament we read about groups of two, 120 and thousands. Which ones were formal? True, in 1 Corinthians 11:18, Paul talks about the people coming together as a church, and he mentions some things they were doing wrong at their assemblies. However, upon examining the whole chapter closely, you will see that Paul is criticizing the assembled for having improper motives. They were divisive (v. 19) and inconsiderate (v. 33). Paul points them back to a heart-level approach to their activities (v. 28).

Notice that although the "whole church" clearly came together, the assembly was not described as formal. We look at the words "whole church," and with our "present mindedness," we are positive that Paul was referring to the "formal gathering of the church," complete with formal dress, opening and closing prayers, and formal announcements at the end. Why "formal"? Maybe "special" would be a better word.

Is the activity a factor in determining formalism? From the Last Supper Jesus had with His apostles in Matthew 26 to the partaking of the Lord's Supper in Acts 20, the emphasis is on simplicity and casualness. We use Acts 20:7 to prove that communion was on the first day of the week, but we ignore golden rays of *koinonia* that permeate the passage. This "first day of the week" assembly was as unstructured and informal as an unplanned reunion of college friends. The important element is that these people were "gathered together"; what they did then is important, but secondary. In that atmosphere, Paul taught them; they shared food; and they refused to break up. Evidently, they didn't have a sundial mounted at the pulpit. In fact, they didn't even have a pulpit.

Are some assembly activities more formal than others? If so, where is the New Testament example? We have seen that the communion was instituted while a meal was being eaten. We are given absolutely no indication that the event was some mysterious, melodramatic ritual, but rather a simple symbolic memorial feast. Granted, we will never fully understand some elements of this sacred feast this side of heaven, but Paul simply said the Lord's Supper is a time to remember (1 Corinthians 11:25), a time to look ahead (v.26), and a time to look within (v.28).

Is there such a thing as a formal prayer as opposed to the "pray without ceasing" Paul advocated? Is singing more formal in the assembly than it is when done by two men in a prison cell? And can collecting the contribution possibly be a formal act when the real act takes place in your heart before the assembly as you considered how God "has prospered" you?

Is the location a determining factor? At this point we need to come to grips with our preference for temple worship. Isn't it generally accepted that assemblies in our buildings are formal, but assemblies elsewhere are informal? The full weight of traditionalism and ritualism are in place when we are in our "sanctuaries," but if we are at a mountain retreat, we feel a sense of freedom and flexibility that would be inappropriate in the sanctuary. If the truth were known, some of our most memorable services take place in wooded chapels, on green hillsides, and around camp-fires. Ask yourself why, and you get answers such as, "It wasn't so formal" and "We had a greater sense of togetherness." God intended for our assemblies to be that way all the time, not just on special occasions.

Using location as a criterion for determining formalism is grossly unbiblical. It smacks of an institutionalism that would have sickened Paul, who met with brethren in homes, in cells, on seashores, and wherever they would listen. *Cathedral mind-sets and temple temperaments have guided our assemblies so long that, even when we can't find it in the Bible, we "just know God meant for it to be that way."*

Are clothes a determining factor? I have often wondered if our assemblies are formal because of the dress clothes we wear or if we dress up because the assemblies are formal. Which causes which? Who decided you should dress up to "go to church"? The Holy Spirit did not direct any of the writers of the New Testament to say that. He did quote Jesus saying, "Is not life more than food, and the body more than clothing? Do not be anxious then, saying, . . . With what shall we clothe ourselves? . . . But seek first His kingdom and His righteousness; and all these things shall be added to you" (Matthew 6:25,31-33). Doesn't requiring, or at least expecting, formal attire for the assemblies smack of elevating the material over the spiritual?

Many have pointed out that Jesus wouldn't be allowed to preach in most of our pulpits because He would be too shabbily dressed. Try preaching without a coat and tie, and see how quickly you join the ranks of the unemployed. Some places even have the audacity to require coats and ties before one can serve communion. They call it appropriate attire. Appropriate to whom?

One of the most twisted, unbiblical and illogical lines of reasoning ever invented goes like this: "We should dress up for church because we should wear our best for God." That statement embodies everything that is wrong about our assemblies. It localizes God, limits worship to a place, disregards Christianity as a way of life, misses the purpose of the assembly, alienates the less fortunate, misleads our children, formalizes the occasion, and emphasizes externals. Other than that, it's a great statement.

Being immodest, inconsiderate and insensitive are always going to be wrong for a child of God whether one is at the assembly or the shopping center. To establish appropriateness beyond that is to create a criterion for judging and ostracizing. Listen to James:

assumes people who may not be dressed

My brethren, do not hold your faith in our glorious Lord Jesus Christ with an attitude of personal favoritism. For if a man comes into your assembly with a gold ring and dressed in fine clothes, and there also comes in a poor man in dirty clothes, and you pay special attention to the one who is wearing the fine clothes, and say, "You sit here in a good place," and you say to the poor man, "You stand over there or sit down by my footstool," have you not made distinctions among yourselves, and become judges with evil motives? (James 2:1-4)

For the sake of trying to "look good" and "put our best foot forward," we have developed a formalism in our assemblies that alienates the disadvantaged, attracts our social equals, and places a burden on those who need love but end up worrying about being accepted. James continued, "Did not God choose the poor of this world to be rich in faith and heirs of the kingdom which He promised to those who love Him?" (v. 5). Maybe the reason we have such a shortage of those who are "rich in faith" is because we have so many who are rich in attire. We live in a country where we believe "clothes make the man," but God says clothes don't make the Christian.

If we have formal assemblies because we wear formal clothes, let's change our clothes. If we wear formal clothes because our assemblies are formal, let's change our assemblies. "So speak and so act, as those who are to be judged by the law of liberty" (v. 12). That is a big difference from taking the liberty to make laws. "For judgment will be merciless to one who has shown no mercy" (v. 13).

Thirdly, how consistent should we be with our formalism?

If we can assume that God wants formalism in our assemblies, isn't it important for us to be consistent? Because formalism is a product of man's imagination, we should have no problem finding that imaginary line called "too formal."

When I was in high school, we understood that we were to wear our best and most formal garb to the senior banquet. So we all ran out, and rented tuxes, bought flowers, and washed the cars we were going to drive. After all, one wouldn't dare drive a dirty car to a banquet. The formal occasion called for formal attire. Now, either church is less important or less formal than that banquet or tuxes are inappropriate for the assembly. Which is it, and what are the determining factors?

Another point of concern for those interested in consistency is the atmosphere of the assembly. Shouldn't we do those things that maximize a formal atmosphere? If so, we need formal music, formal prayers, formal language, formal attire for leaders, and formal surroundings. "Well, that's too formal," someone says. "It sounds like the high church services some religious groups have." Why would incorporating these things be too formal? When we dropped back from being like that, who decided to stop at the level we did?

The point is not to be facetious, but to help us see that our assemblies are the result of arbitrary decisions rather than a desire to copy the New Testament church. This thought brings me to the last question.

Fourth, using the New Testament as your guide, describe a typical-first century assembly of Christians.

I have dealt with the scarcity of passages on the topic, but now I am asking you to take a serious look at New Testament assemblies. Use Acts 2:42-47, Acts 20:6-12, and 1 Corinthians 11-14 to get an overview of what the early Christians did. Take some time to write out what the common elements were and what the atmosphere seemed to be like.

When you look at them without any preconceived notions, you see the embodiment of what God called for over and over again. Jesus said it (Matthew 22:34-40), Paul said it (Romans 13:8-10), James said it (James 2:5-8). His children are to love Him and one another, and that sums up the law. That is exactly what you see, sins and misunderstandings aside, when you examine the assemblies of the early church. They focused on Jesus and His Word and emphasized togetherness. You see a relaxed, informal atmosphere of love, sharing and upbuilding.

Their assemblies seem to have been orderly, but not tightly structured. In Acts 2, the daily togetherness is emphasized. In Acts 20, they "were gathered together to break bread" and talked all night. In 1 Corinthians 11-14, fellowship or *koinonia* was the dominating element. The early church had some serious problems, but those problems were matters of the heart more than rules of order. The atmosphere was one of the home and family, not social or religious duty and obligation. We see in those Christians a deep commitment to drawing closer to God and each other. In other words, their emphasis was on the growing of godly relationships, not the fulfilling of external requirements.

Paul echoed these sentiments when he wrote to the Colossian brethren. He was talking about all the Christians who would never get to hear him personally, folks like you and me, when he said,

> For I want you to know how great a struggle I have on your behalf, and for those who are at Laodicea, and for all those who have not personally seen my face, that their hearts may be knit together in love, and attaining to all the wealth that comes from the full assurance of understanding, resulting in a true knowledge of God's mystery, that is, Christ Himself. (Colossians 2:1,2)

New Testament Christians assembled in order to bring about the knitting together of their hearts in love through Jesus Christ. God gave them some tools to assist them in that knitting process. They kept no rituals, acts, traditions or obligations – except to help one another grow in love.

The remainder of this book will focus on what they did when they came together. Some specific objectives needed to be accomplished in order to bring about the knitting of hearts. Those objectives included encouragement, equipping and enjoyment; those things would lead to evangelism. We must develop a willingness to change the emphasis in our assembly.

DISCUSSION QUESTIONS

1. Is formalism in the assembly a biblical principle or a traditional/cultural preference?

2. What are the advantages and disadvantages of keeping the assembly formal (that is, structured, somber, formal attire)?

3. What determines whether an assembly is formal or informal? Size? Time? Location?

4. Why are devotionals, retreats, sunrise services and mountain top assemblies so special and meaningful?

5. Why do we dress up to be together on Sunday? Does it unite or alienate? Is our dress consistent with Matthew 6:25-33 and James 2:1-6?

SECTION TWO
ENCOURAGEMENT
AND THE ASSEMBLY

CHAPTER SIX
Don't Change That Channel

Have you ever given a death notification? As a volunteer police chaplain, I have had to be the bearer of terrible news a couple of hundred times. The first responsibility after the notification has been made is to help persons cope with their grief. After the initial shock has subsided, I call for reinforcements. I contact their minister, relatives and friends because no one should endure pain alone. The saddest death notifications I have ever been a part of are not the saddest because of the tragedy, but because there was no one to call to help. The person who received the sad news was alone.

Mosie Lister wrote a very moving song that never fails to bring a tear to my eye when we sing it. It's titled "Where No One Stands Alone," and the second verse especially catches in my throat.

Like a king I may live in a palace so tall,
With great riches to call my own;
But I don't know a thing in this whole wide world
That's worse than being alone.

Chorus:

Hold my hand all the way, every hour, every day,
From here to the great unknown.
Take my hand: Let me stand
Where no one stands alone.[17]

When God stepped back to review His creation, He was impressed with what He saw: lush vegetation, colorful fruits, pure flowing rivers, and a multitude of coexisting animals. Everything was beautiful and gloriously reflected the majesty of its Creator – everything, that is, except man. Man was incomplete.

One little Sunday school student described Adam as a "twink." "A what?" asked the astonished teacher. "That's a Twinkie with only one in the package. There's supposed to be two," answered the youngster, surprised that he had to explain it.

When God looked at man, He made a comment that has remained true throughout the ages. "It is not good for the man to be alone" (Genesis 2:18). Why, then, should it be a surprise that He wants His children to be together? Every analogy God used to describe the church emphasizes togetherness. The church is a family, a body, a tree, and a bride, just to name a few. Each of these concepts is a variation on the same theme – togetherness.

A few years ago, the police called me and asked me to help with a potential suicide case. Within minutes I was sitting a few feet away from a young girl who held a knife to her stomach and threatened to kill herself if I came any closer. After sharing her problems with me, she finally handed me the knife and said, "I guess I really wasn't going to kill myself. I just wanted someone to listen to me." Those words bore their way into my heart as I understood for the first time how devastating loneliness can be to a person. Even people with families, jobs and churches can be terribly lonely.

The saddest indictment of any church is that it is structured in such a way that members can attend the assembly and still be alone. Something desperately needs to change when that can happen. But that thought brings us to another sacred cow: change. If the church needs to change and God is expecting change, what does it say about us when we refuse to change?

Several years ago, I removed the lectern from our auditorium. I wanted to be closer to the audience when I spoke, and the lectern was a barrier. The only purpose for its existence was a practical one: It was a place to lay my notes. As a neophyte preacher, it also hid my shaking knees, but that was years ago. Now I have my notes in my Bible, and my knees don't shake. So I got rid of it.

Removing the lectern was seen by all merely as an act of expediency, right? Wrong. The congregation accepted it readily, but to some visitors I had removed a piece of religious furniture. It had become a surrogate idol to folks who vowed they had no idols.

One older fellow who visited with us shook my hand as he went out the door. Instead of the usual

"Good sermon, Preacher," he looked me in the eye, stuck his jaw out, and said, "If you folks can't afford a pulpit, I'll buy you one!" He was very disturbed; I was completely dumfounded. I am convinced he was reacting to a change that somehow threatened him. You'd have thought I'd replaced the Bible with *Playboy* magazine instead of removing a piece of obsolete furniture.

Few things betray our loyalty to tradition like a suggestion to make a change in the assembly. Upon hearing such a suggestion, the fur flies – not faith, just fur. We will change nearly everything else in our lives in an attempt to improve or even just because we need a change, but if we change the assembly any, brotherly love becomes an archaic concept.

Why? Listed below are some reasons why folks don't like change in the assembly.

First, religion is a habit. When I get up in the morning, I stumble into the kitchen and fix a cup of coffee while my brain continues to sleep. What really messes the system up is to be going through these usually thoughtless motions only to discover that the coffee can is empty. Then I have to wake up, find a new can of coffee in the pantry, open it up on our cantankerous can opener, and then continue fixing the coffee. I am forced to think about something I don't want to think about. It is easier just to go through the habitual motions.

When you change things in the assembly, people have to stop and think about it. No longer is it only 2+2=4, but why does 2+2=4? God deplores thoughtless religion.

Second, people are satisfied with the status quo. The common excuse is "Don't change a good thing."

Good for whom? Something is terribly wrong with any Christian who is satisfied with his or her spiritual condition. Grace is awesome, and there is power in the blood, but God's people are always in the process of becoming better Christians. That is what growth is all about. "Grow in the grace and knowledge of our Lord Jesus Christ," said Peter, because we are, or should be, unsatisfied with ourselves. We "hunger and thirst after righteousness" because we want to grow. If we are spiritually "fat and happy," where is the desire to improve?

Third, people don't like to challenge their faith. To challenge one's faith is to be confronted by one's lack of faith. Who wants that? If we have to start re-looking, re-examining, and re-thinking, we might find that we are a lot like the rich young ruler, who was expecting to be reaffirmed by Jesus, but who "went away grieved" when his faith was challenged (Matthew 19:16-22).

I have said in many sermons, "Jesus came to hassle our castle." He told us we would be in a state of constant turmoil because of our commitment to Him. After describing the depth of God's concern for us, He called on His disciples to "confess Me before men." He knew that confession would cause some problems in our lives.

> Do not think that I came to bring peace on the earth; I did not come to bring peace, but a sword. For I came to set a man against his father, and a daughter against her mother, and a daughter-in-law against her mother-in-law; and a man's enemies will be the members of his household. He who loves father or mother more than Me is not worthy of Me; and he who loves son or daughter more than Me is not worthy of Me. And he

who does not take his cross and follow after Me is not worthy of Me. He who has found his life shall lose it, and he who has lost his life for My sake shall find it. (Matthew 10:34-39)

Our faith is an ever-changing thing because it is an always-growing thing. To stand still is to stagnate and die. Paul said that we were all "being transformed into the same image from glory to glory, just as from the Lord" (2 Corinthians 3:18). "Transformed" means to change, and change can be painful. Yet the Bible is replete with calls for the child of God to examine, test and question his faith. Why? "That the proof of your faith, being more precious than gold which is perishable, even though tested by fire, may be found to result in praise and glory and honor at the revelation of Jesus Christ" (1 Peter 1:7). We can be unchanged to the bitter end, or we can change for a better end.

Graham Kendrick summed it up nicely when he wrote:

If we are to make progress in our worship, there is no escaping the prospect of change. With change comes conflict, and we are afraid of both. If however, we want to avoid change and conflict, then we must of necessity avoid Christ as well, because his kingdom only grows as his people radically change to become like him, and the stronger it gets the more it conflicts with rival kingdoms, whether of men or of Satan.[18]

Fourth, sometimes it is easier to be faithful to a structure instead of a Savior. Every church has its own way of doing things in the assembly. Whether it is having two songs and a prayer or having the Lord's Supper before the sermon instead of after, we like our

66

way of doing things. Some churches have huge productions, and others are informal and casual. Some structure comes from necessity, some from expediency, and some as a matter of doctrine. But who knows, and does anybody care? We've got the "way" but not the whys. Why do we do things the way we do them? Is it the best way? Is it the most productive way? Is it the most relevant and scriptural way?

"We've done it this way for 50 years, and we don't need to change it now," says the all-too-familiar voice of tradition. Such a statement offers no explanation or point to rebut, just an unqualified commitment to the tried-and-true structure. Instead of being a tool to bring us closer to Jesus, structure takes His place. Sadly enough, sometimes the structure we've created is given more loyalty than the Creator who made us. Paul's judgment of the Gentiles might be applicable in some religious circles today. He said they had "exchanged the truth of God for a lie, and worshiped and served the creature rather than the Creator" (Romans 1:25).

We may give some security in unchangeable structure, but our security is supposed to rest on the eternal and unchangeable Savior of our souls. If our unity is based on having Jesus in common, change and growth are inevitable. But if the only thing we have in common is structure, then weakness and loneliness are inevitable.

So what's the point? We started out describing how terrible it is to be alone, and we went directly to the need for change. The connection should be obvious. When God saw that man was alone and it wasn't good, He changed things to make them better. For us to allow a situation to continue in our assembly where someone could attend, be a member, and still be alone is unthinkable. We must change things to correct the problem. Actually, we need to return to God's original plan for the assembly. The assembly is a togetherness event, not a legalistic obligation. Church assemblies have become such formal productions that we have developed what Paul warned the early church of – a "form of godliness (and) denied its power" (2 Timothy 3:5). Form is check-list structure, but power is a life-changing, heart-level experience. Which did God intend for us to have? What did the early Christians have in their assemblies – form or power?

Form says we assemble because we are required to. Power says we assemble because we need to be together and draw more power from each other and from the Holy Spirit. Form says we assemble to perform rituals. Power says we assemble to build one another up. Form emphasizes attendance. Power emphasizes togetherness. Form says, "Go to church." Power says, "Have the mind of Christ."

Thoughtless rituals in mindless assemblies truly must hurt God. The giving of His Son was the zenith of love; in return He gets zombie love. *Folks are sitting in our assemblies hurting with problems and aching for someone to care, but what they get is form, frowns and farewells.* They are supposed to feel good because they "went to church," but what they feel is alone. Something needs to change. Something is missing.

DISCUSSION QUESTIONS

1. Are your assemblies structured to encourage

interaction, or is it possible for someone to attend and never talk to another Christian?

2. How willing are you to accept change? How would you feel if the lectern or communion table were removed? How would you feel about changing the pews for chairs, or instead of two assemblies on Sunday, having one longer assembly in the afternoon?

3. What are some of the reasons why people don't like change?

4. What could you change about your assembly to ensure that no one was alone?

5. Why do you attend the assembly of the church?

CHAPTER SEVEN
Thanks, I Needed That

One of the greatest changes we can make in our assemblies is to return to one of the primary purposes for the assembly in New Testament times. The early Christians came together in order to encourage one another.

A few years ago, I ran in my first 10K race. Actually, it was not a race for me in that I was not competing with anyone. My objectives were to stay alive, finish the race, and not choke to death on the other runners' trail dust. The biggest surprise of the entire event was finding some obstacles that where never present on my practice course hills.

Two miles into the race, my legs became spaghetti and my tongue kept getting in the way of my feet. If my brain hadn't been so tired, I'm sure my life would have been flashing before my eyes. As it was, my mind was in a freeze frame mode with the picture of that glass of water I had earlier poured out on the ground. I was worse than Esau. I'd have sold my birthright for one cup of water.

Plodding around a bend in the road, I could see a table ahead. As I drew closer to the table, it seemed to be covered with cups of water – clear, cold water. Before me was a feast for a king. I grabbed one of the cups as I zoomed past at the speed of night and gulped the water down, paper cup and all. I was so refreshed and invigorated that I actually picked up the pace. Just when I was giving out again, another drink table was set up at the three-and-a-half-mile point. Then there was one at the five-and-a-half mile point, which gave me enough of a boost to finish the entire 6.2 miles. I would have never finished the race if those little cups of water hadn't been given at just the right time.

Encouragement is like cups of water given at just the right times. In the mad marathon of life, spirits get weak and souls become thirsty. Church is a serving table surrounded by people passing out cups of encouragement to all who come by. Just when you think you can't go another step, you come to a loving, giving person who dispenses the encouragement you need to help you stay in the race. This act gives a whole new meaning to Jesus' message in Mark 9:41. Even though Jesus was giving a warning to His disciples about not hindering good works, the passage always causes me to think of 10Ks and encouragement.

He said,

For whoever gives you a cup of water to drink because of your name as followers of Christ, truly I say to you, he shall not lose his reward.

Encouragement sustains, revives, builds up, strokes, fortifies, inspires, comforts and cheers. Encouragement is the glue that keeps us close, the rah-rah that keeps us going, and the hook that keeps us coming back for more. It's a drug we can't get enough of and a gift that we never tire of giving. Encouragement is brotherly love in action and Christlike in attitude. One of the main reasons Christians assemble is for encouragement. It's what people do when they care about one another.

David went from being the hero of Israel to a hunted fugitive. Saul was crazy with jealousy and determined to kill the young upstart who the people claimed was 10 times the commander Saul was. Cut off from family and friends and running for his life, David needed a shot in the arm. "And Jonathan, Saul's son, arose and went to David at Horesh, and encouraged him in God" (1 Samuel 23:16). That's what people do when they care about each other. Encouragement not only turns lives around, but it also sustains when life showers us with spears.

Nothing plunges a congregation into despair like the death of a member. The hurt is shared by all the members as they embrace, weep and comfort one another. Even those who know better ask, "Why did it have to happen?" and "What is going to happen to him now?" The brethren in Thessalonica were asking those very questions about these of their number who were "asleep." Paul told them to remember the hope they had through Christ. When the Lord comes again, we and all those who have died in the Lord will be taken up to meet Him. "Therefore, comfort one another with these words." Then he added, "encourage one another, and build up one another" (1 Thessalonians 4:13 – 5:11).

Encouragement is not icing on the cake; it *is* the cake. Somehow we have seen the assembly as a requirement to be fulfilled, a duty to perform, and a command to be obeyed. If you happen to be encouraged by the assembly, your experience is just a serendipity. That idea is not the way the Bible describes the assembly. We assemble for the purpose of encouraging one another. If we miss the assembly, we miss the opportunity to give and receive encouragement.

THE ELEVENTH COMMANDMENT

As a teenage Christian, I once got into a debate about the Ten Commandments (the tablets, not the movie). I just knew that one of the commandments was "Forsake not the assembling of yourselves together." I was completely shocked when I learned that I was wrong. I had heard the phrase preached so forcefully, commandingly and regularly that I'd assumed it was one of the original Ten. That verse made church attendance mandatory, so it was presented as cut-and-dry dogma. No explanations were necessary because the command was so emphatic. "You will go to church. You will not miss for any reason short of death. You will not question the whys and wherefores of this topic."

Few passages of the Bible have been more abused and misused than Hebrews 10:25. Such misuse is a classic example of using a verse as a club to beat the masses into external faithfulness. Viewing the verse this way is the natural result of going to the Bible to find laws and not the principles that undergird them.

The Hebrew writer was not laying down a series of edicts or laws, but rather was pointing out the need for Christians to be together. Because we are part of "a new and living way" (v. 20), we must build on that newness by keeping our hearts and consciences clean. To do this, the writer says,

> Let us hold fast the confession of our hope without wavering, for He who promised is faithful; and let us consider how to stimulate one another to love and good deeds, not forsaking our own assembling together, as is the habit of some, but encouraging one another; and all the more, as you see the day drawing near. (v. 23-25)

One does not have to be a scholar to recognize that faithfulness to the assembly is part of what's being discussed in this passage. What has been overlooked is the reason one needs to assemble. The topic of this passage is Christians encouraging Christians, and a good part of that takes place in the assembly. We actually need to be thinking of ways to encourage or stimulate each other to love and service. The real concern of this section is that if one misses the assembly, one misses out on all the encouraging that takes place.

Two aspects of this passage should disturb all of us. One is the use of a phrase to brow-beat Christians into attending church. The other is the emphasis on encouragement as a dominant element in the assembly. Sometimes we do a lot of "stirring up" in our assemblies, but it's not "to love and good deeds." I have heard folks judge their assembly based on the degree of discomfort they felt, as if the assembly was some kind of punishment or penance. *The toe-stomping, hand-slapping, hell-fire-and-brimstone preaching may make people feel as if they've paid for their sins because they endured the service, but what they needed was simple, compassionate encouragement.* The idea, according to Hebrews, is to leave the assembly charged up with love and anxious to do good deeds.

Obviously we must find a balance between the need to rebuke and convict and the need to encourage and build up. The point is that Hebrews 10:25 is used as a club when the context is dealing with encouragement.

The good folks at Corinth were mired in misunderstanding and swamped by selfish pursuits. In getting them to clean up their act, Paul called them back to the foundational principle of Christian togetherness. "Let all things be done for edification" (1 Corinthians 14:26). Everyone has preferences and pet peeves, but these must be held in check to meet the greater need of building up one another. From the very beginning, it seems that the Lord's church has tended to forget why they come together.

Hebrews 10:19-25 is one of the most exciting and profound descriptions of Christian togetherness found in the Bible. To reduce it to a piece of religious legislation is to rob it of its meaning and its purpose. The writer says we can confidently approach God through Jesus because we are part of a "new and living way."

This thrilling new relationship is based on the sincerity of our hearts and the cleansing of our lives. We are sure of our faith as we firmly place ourselves in His hands. As a result, we constantly look for opportunities to help other Christians grow in love and deeds. To build up one another is why we need to be together and why we should try to never miss a chance to encourage one another.

Depending on how you read it, the writer may be more concerned with the missed opportunity to give encouragement than he is with mere attendance. The whole tenor of the passage is that encouragement comes from a heart overflowing with love and thankfulness, a heart that desperately wants to help others avoid the judgment of God (v. 26-31).

Encouragement must be an integral part of the Christian's life and assembly, not an optional element to be discarded in the rush to "get the important things done first." Encouragement must be more than a "hit or miss" part of our assemblies, and it must be more than an occasional sermon about Barnabas.

Can you imagine what a difference it would make in our assemblies if we consciously sought the most effective ways to encourage one another. I can hear people protesting, "But I am encouraged by our assemblies!" Wonderful, but is it not more a serendipity than an objective? We go through our check list of rituals, and if you happen to be a little encouraged in the process, good, but that is incidental to what we want to accomplish. Encouragement is not incidental in Hebrews 10:19-25. It is a reason, an aim, an objective and a goal. More important, encouraging one another is authentic Christlikeness.

PEOPLE POWER

We should not be surprised that encouragement has a prominent role in the assembly. The surprise is the fact that we have to be reminded of its importance. If we claim to be Christ's church, we need to start acting like Christ. In His earthly ministry, He was the embodiment of encouragement. From performing the miracle in Cana to speaking to the thief on the cross, Jesus, with one exception, actively encouraged all who would listen to Him. The recorded encounters He had with individuals are touching stories of shared love and cheered spirits. He was concerned with helping, healing, picking up, washing feet, serving, comforting and saving. He encouraged because He was moved with compassion. The exception to this behavior came when He scorned the religious who were too busy splitting hairs, drawing lines, and carving up hearts to do any encouraging.

Many times, after the official "closing prayer," which closes out the "formal" assembly, members scurry to grab the deacon who forgot to get the light bulbs replaced; the song leader, who let the songs drag; Sister Ann, who came in too late again; the preacher, who used a wrong reference; the sound engineer, who had the volume too low; Brother Joe, who forgot to lower the thermostat; the teens who were passing notes; and so it goes. The assembly has gone from "Amazing Grace" to amazing gripes. The aisles and foyer become battlegrounds for critics, nitpickers and legal eagles. The weak are berated; those responsible are corrected; and the few who were inspired are deflated.

Instead of a peak experience, the assembly becomes

a pecking experience as brethren fume and feign righteous indignation. The majority are thinking more about roast than righteousness, so there is no one available to hand out encouragements. So folks go home having missed out on strokes both during and after the assembly. But then, they got what they expected. These attitudes certainly are not prevalent everywhere every time, but haven't you been in assemblies where this accurately portrays the atmosphere?

A few years ago, a simple little book took the business world by storm and became a best seller. The compact book presented a threefold approach to the successful management of people. It suggested setting one-minute goals, giving one-minute praisings, and offering one-minute reprimands. Following these suggestions resulted in greater productivity, a happier work environment, and made one *The One Minute Manager*. The authors of this popular book emphatically made it clear that encouragement was an essential part of success. They were coming from a purely business managerial viewpoint without any religious intent. Yet, they saw encouragement as essential in bringing the best out of people. In giving a very brief summary of their "game plan" they said, " . . . to give yourself and others the gift of getting greater results in less time, set goals; praise and reprimand behaviors; encourage people; speak the truth; laugh; work; enjoy and encourage the people you work with to do the same as you do!"[19]

It is amazing to see how crucial encouragement is to their entire "game plan." The authors simply recognize an elementary aspect of human nature, which is that people respond better to encouragement than to anything else.

Experience and common sense tell us that building people up gets positive results, and tearing them down gets negative results and down people. The call for us to be Christlike is a call for us to be encouragers. Listen to Paul in Ephesians 4:

> But speaking the truth in love, we are to grow up in all aspects into Him, who is the head, even Christ . . . .
> Be renewed in the spirit of your mind, and put on the new self, which in the likeness of God has been created in righteousness and holiness of the truth. Therefore, laying aside falsehood, speak truth, each one of you, with his neighbor, for we are members of one another . . . .
> Let no unwholesome word proceed from your mouth, but only such a word as is good for edification according to the need of the moment, that it may give grace to those who hear . . . .
> Let all bitterness and wrath and anger and clamor and slander be put away from you, along with malice. And be kind to one another, tender-hearted, forgiving each other, just as God in Christ also has forgiven you. (v. 15,23-25,29,31,32)

For these things to take place, Christians have to be together. Hence, one of the primary purposes of the assembly is to provide an opportunity for us to encourage one another in the Lord. In other words, the assembly is, or should be, an encouraging experience. The assembly is people, who out of love and loyalty to Christ, interact in such a way so as to build one another up spiritually. Sadly enough, if you want to be where discouraging words are seldom heard, you have to go where the deer and the antelope play, not church.

DISCUSSION QUESTIONS

1. How can the assembly be used to "stir one another up to love and good deeds"?

2. According to Hebrews 10:23-25, why should we make every effort to attend the assembly?

3. What is the foundational principle of Christian togetherness, according to 1 Corinthians 14:26?

4. Is encouragement a serendipity or an objective in your assemblies?

5. Do you respond better to encouragement or guilt? Are they mutually exclusive forms of motivation?

CHAPTER EIGHT
Meet Me On Cloud Nine

Occasionally something is encouraging simply because it is not discouraging. But encouragement should be more than that. Some characteristics are inherently understood when one thinks about encouragement.

First, encouragement is active. Encouragement is purposeful, directed and self-initiated. For encouragement to take place, someone has to take some action. Even accidental encouragement results from action. So when we talk about encouragement as being part of the assembly, we are recognizing that someone, or ones, must make it happen, take the initiative, and be a catalyst.

Second, encouragement is unselfish. Those

engrossed in their own egos are rarely the source of encouragement to others. Barnabas was the "Son of Encouragement" because he unselfishly gave of himself and his possessions. Jesus was a constant encourager, and He showed us that we must be others oriented. To follow Him we must deny self and live for Him by caring for "the least of these." A church that places top priority on encouragement is a church that is unselfish.

Third, encouragement is verbal. I know encouragement can be a quiet act of love, a warm hug, or pat on the back. But encouragement has its roots in verbal expressions of inspiration and comfort. Remember the words of Solomon? "Like apples of gold in settings of silver is a word spoken in right circumstances" (Proverbs 25:11). All three of the primary Greek words used in the New Testament for encouragement refer to verbal interaction. While encouraging can certainly be something you do, it is mainly a matter of what you say.[20] That simply means there must be interaction and communication for maximum encouragement to take place.

Finally, and most obviously, encouragement is uplifting. It builds up, picks up and revs up. As a close look at the word reveals, it fortifies the recipients' courage. It provides the needed strength to keep on keeping on. It turns failures into learning experiences, quitters into fighters, and marginal Christians into spiritual leaders. Encouragement makes the assembly a good deal instead of an ordeal.

Now take a few moments and reflect on these four elements of encouragement: active, unselfish, verbal, uplifting. To what extent do you see these characteristics in your assembly?

It appears to me that the structure of our assemblies is such that each of these elements is either inappropriate or very minimal. *Encouragement is active, but the structure of the assembly is passive.* ("We expect everyone to participate as long as they shut up and sit still.") The leaders are active, but for the most part, everyone else is a spectator.

Encouragement is unselfish, giving and sharing, but our assemblies call for each person to be introspective. We find our quiet little corner and meditate. After all, isn't religion a personal matter – even when you are together with the church? And aren't we supposed to treat our assemblies as solemn occasions? We are all so quiet and contemplative. If encouragement is verbal, then it must be the job of the preacher because he is the only one permitted to speak above a whisper.

Encouragement is uplifting, so if our assemblies are uplifting, they must also be encouraging. Maybe, but attaining this goal is a hit-and-miss proposition at best. We hope our assemblies are uplifting, but the sad truth is that most assemblies are long on structure and short on substance. Folks are crying for closeness, but what they get is a program of the services.

Is interaction out of the question? Are warm greetings only appropriate in the foyer? Would it be out of place to have a period of person-to-person encouragement? Maybe a format more like one of our Bible classes would work.

Graham Kendrick tells a story about a little boy's first trip to church with his mother. She scrubbed him clean and dressed him in his "Sunday best." Then he was warned firmly to be on his best behavior and to stay close by his mother. His curiosity was running wild as they slipped into the huge building and onto an empty pew. He noticed that his mother sat in silence with her head bowed low. Naturally, he tried to imitate her actions, but after a brief period, the question that had been eating at him since they entered the building exploded from his lips for all to hear. "Mummy, who are we all hiding from?"[21]

Somehow, I don't believe he was very encouraged by the response his mother gave. The uncluttered eye of youth saw the paradox of coming together so we can be all alone. We do gain encouragement from meditation and introspective searching, but the purpose of being together is to revel in spiritual intimacy and grow through mutual upbuilding. Encouragement is not optional equipment but standard on all New Testament models.

PLANNED OR ACCIDENTAL

"Stop right there! Prayer is encouraging. So whenever someone leads a prayer in the assembly, it is encouraging." We would like to think that, but in reality encouraging prayer usually depends on the abilities of the one leading the prayer. From those who mumble through their prayer to those who preach sermons in their prayers, we sometimes have difficulty concentrating and feeling encouraged by what is said. Because we all have our heads bowed, does that make it a "one-another" experience?

"Well, giving has to be an encouraging part of the assembly. After all it is an unselfish act." Giving is unselfish, but the purpose was to have taken place in the heart long before the collection took place (2 Cor-

86

inthians 9:7). The collection is just an expediency. The important thing is that churches give themselves to the Lord (2 Corinthians 8:5). That would be encouraging, just as it was to Paul when he wrote about the Macedonian brethren. The question we need to think about is: "How can we make the contribution an encouraging experience?" The Lord loves a cheerful giver, and I suspect brethren would, too.

Sitting at a dinner table communing with His disciples, Jesus took a piece of bread and a cup of wine and instituted what we call the Lord's Supper. This simple memorial feast was to serve as a reminder of His death, His return, and our commitment to Him (1 Corinthians 11:23-29). The Bible calls the feast *koinonia*, fellowship or communion and it is the very essence of togetherness. Sure the Supper is personal, but the New Testament church had to come together to do it (Acts 20:7). Yet today we have made it a completely private matter as we each pull into our formal fetal position and meditate. We must examine ourselves – the Bible tells us to – but we need to put *koinonia* back into the Lord's Supper somehow. We pass up an opportunity to do some first class encouraging because we are all spiritually sequestered through the entire thing. The level of encouragement is determined by one's ability to concentrate and not by the amount of *koinonia* taking place.

Singing should always be an encouraging, one-another experience. Paul said that we should be "teaching and admonishing one another with psalms and hymns and spiritual songs, singing with thankfulness in your hearts to God" (Colossians 3:16). While singing is clearly a togetherness act, the level of encouragement is somewhat dependent on the quality of the singing and the type of songs sung. Many times songs are used more for fillers than sources of encouragement. A song is what you have before the prayer, after the sermon, and between the contribution and Lord's Supper. We sing to teach and admonish one another, but many times the singing is reduced to another meaningless requirement.

The largest chunk of the assembly is usually reserved for the sermon. Even allowing for enthusiastic listeners, preaching continues to be one-way communication with passive receivers and unmeasurable results. The sermon may be encouraging or it may be depressing. *A steady diet of tongue lashings or verbal valium can make even the most dedicated Christians groan when the preacher mounts the pulpit.* Again, encouragement is dependent on one individual's talents or particular bent rather than being an inseparable part of the assembly.

I enjoy fishing – when the fish are biting. In spite of the nice weather and the beauties of nature, if the fish aren't biting, I am ready to change sports. But, I have sat in a deer stand for 10 hours waiting for my next taxidermy bill to walk by. The difference is interest and expectations. I expect fish to bite, but I know if that monster buck comes by, it will be largely because of luck. It helps to absolutely love deer hunting whether or not I ever shoot a deer. If I wanted to be assured of catching fish, I would go to a place where the water is stocked with fish. At trout farms and catfish farms, one intends and expects to catch fish.

Having encouragement in the assembly must not be left to a matter of luck or good timing. It must be like the trout farm where a big catch is expected and designed to happen. When Christians have to take a trip down Memory Lane to remember the last time an assembly was encouraging, it is time to restock the pond.

As the late Andy T. Richie Jr. said in his classic book *Thou Shalt Worship The Lord Thy God*:

> The scope of meaningful worship is very broad. Purity of purpose is of supreme importance. What we include is just as vital, if not more so, as what we exclude. Leaving out warmth and sincerity and purpose could be as devastating to some as allowing unauthorized practices to slip in. On the one hand we could be condemned for presumptuous additions, but on the other we could starve ourselves if we do not truly feed on the "Bread of Life" and drink of the "Water of Life."[22]

The "Bread of Life" and the "Water of Life" are the spirit of Christ, the spirit that His followers share and give to each other every chance they have to be together.

The question that should be on our lips is, How can we maximize encouragement in our assemblies? To a large extent, the answer will depend on the needs and the character of your congregation. Look again at the New Testament church. Notice the commitment to togetherness. Those Christians did not seem to have any concerns about time frames, formalities, special facilities, routines, or how the church in the next town acted in its assemblies. They had no one to copy and only Christ to please. They were guided by the overriding principle, "Let all things be done for edification." We must always remain loyal to the Word and sensitive to the feelings and expectations of our brethren, but God has given us a great deal of freedom when it comes to how we use the assembly. The opportunities for incorporating encouragement into all we do are limitless.

Why should we be so concerned about the level of encouragement in the assembly? Because we are interested in faith, not facades. We exist for people, not programs. *We know that the only thing that serves as our credential to the world as disciples of Christ is the love we have and show for one another.* Also, as the Hebrew writer said, we need to be "encouraging one another; and all the more, as you see the day drawing near." Because we face that approaching day, we cannot afford to waste an opportunity to encourage one another.

DISCUSSION QUESTIONS

1. What are some of the inherent elements of encouragement?

2. Would you describe your role in the assembly as active or passive? Why?

3. Is the assembly a positive or negative experience for children? What do we expect them to receive from attending?

4. How can praying, singing, giving, preaching and communion be made more encouraging?

5. When does the world see us "love one another" and thus discover that we are His disciples? Would they learn that in your assembly?

SECTION THREE
EQUIPPING
AND THE ASSEMBLY

CHAPTER NINE
Loaded For Bear

Playing football for a small, private high school had several disadvantages. One of the biggest problems was ill-fitting equipment. The school was too poor to offer a wide selection of sizes, so we had to wear whatever was given to us by the coach. As a result, I had shoulder pads that made me look more like an airplane than a lineman. I think the coach hoped those pads would make me look like the huge guard I was supposed to be but wasn't. The shoulder pads sure made it difficult to run, but occasionally, if I caught a strong breeze, I could glide down the field. This run was helped by thigh pads that looked more like sails than protective padding.

The worst piece of equipment I had was an enormous helmet, which was fitted with one of the new lineman's face-guards called cages. While the cage stopped many a forearm, thus saving my nose, it made the helmet so front heavy that I had to hold it up when I ran. I am sure it did little to intimidate my opponents when I got into my three-point stance and then used my free left hand to lift up my helmet in order to look them in the eyes. On several occasions I thought I was unconscious when actually my helmet had been knocked down over my eyes. I found it difficult to be good when I had poor equipment.

I am thankful that our Father has given me the best equipment as I compete for the crown of life. He said that I have been completely equipped for every good work and I have everything necessary for life and godliness. He has taken good care of me. He wants me to win and receive the rewards that He has prepared for those on His team.

God is the great equipper. He has given us His Word as a lamp to guide us. We have His Holy Spirit to comfort, lead and intercede for us. We can talk to Him anytime, anywhere and about anything. And He has given us the best kind of support system there is – a family, the church. We must assemble together to encourage and equip one another.

"Just a second," someone protests. "We don't assemble to equip. We assemble to praise God." That's true if you mean that God is praised by our obedience or that someone is admonished because of our singing the praises of God. If you mean praising God through statements directed toward Him in addition to prayer, you are referring to an Old Testament approach to praise. In the New Testament, praise is redefined as our lives. Praising God is not something you perform, it is something you are. We live to His praise (Ephesians 1:12); we do all to His glory (1 Corinthians 10:31); and we do all in the name of His Son (Colossians 3:17). God is praised anytime we are obedient to Him, not because we all get together and say, "Praise God."

God is not a mass of ego sitting up in heaven soaking up all the praise and adoration we can send His way. He does not need our praise. He wants our hearts. This is what Paul was trying to get the Mars Hill mob to understand when he said,

> The God who made the world and all things in it, since He is the Lord of heaven and earth, does not dwell in temples made with hands; neither is He served by human hands, as though He needed anything, since He Himself gives to all life and breath and all things. (Acts 17:24,25)

We have come to believe that going to church is something we do for God. "It's the least we can do for Him after all He has done for us," some think. Assembling together *is* being obedient to God, but we must understand that God wants us to assemble because *we* need it. We need to be encouraged. We need to be better equipped. *As long as going to church is seen as paying our spiritual dues, it will never bring about the kind of spiritual growth God intended.*

Must one go to church to commune with God? No, but one must assemble to commune with the saints. Must one go to church to express love for God? No. Love for God is expressed by loving our brethren and keeping His commandments (1 John 4:7-21). Must one go to church to be properly equipped? Yes, if the assembly is geared to making sure that equipping takes place.

Equipping is hands-on learning, which results in both spiritual and numerical growth. Aside from several other considerations, this explains why ritual-oriented assemblies are so disastrous, why boring services are so deadly, and why form and formalism can be so damning. No one is being equipped; they are just present and accounted for. If we assemble, yet fail to equip one another to better serve and better imitate Christ, what are we doing? Generally, we reconfirm our prejudices, reaffirm our orthodoxy, and re-establish church attendance as the primary activity of Christians.

When we sing "Give me that old time religion," we don't mean help me draw closer to the Jesus I read about in the Bible. We mean tell me I am right about what I already believe, and that our way is the best way. Who needs equipping when you already have everything you need?

CHANGING WHEELS

We have a double-car garage, but we haven't had a car in it for years. Part of the reason for that is because of the number of bicycles parked in it. We could open a used bike store with all the two-wheelers we have. They range from a tiny dirt bike to a large adult sized 10-speed, with assorted girls' bikes in the middle.

When my children started riding bikes, they had small ones equipped with training wheels. Even then they wobbled and jerked as they maneuvered the bikes up and down the sidewalk. Back then, a two inch bump in the sidewalk made them panic. They grew and felt confident with their small bikes, but longed for the day when the training wheels could be removed. When I finally took the training wheels off, it seemed that the next day they were talking about wanting bigger bikes.

As their bodies grew, their need for a bigger challenge grew, too. Now they zoom all over the neighborhood exploring, visiting and growing even more. The new bikes that seemed complicated and scary are handled with ease and as second nature.

Those small bikes and training wheels served a purpose. In fact, the children could use them now if they wanted, but those bikes would be slow and uncomfortable for them, and I am sure they would be permanently parked before long. But, I am glad they don't use them. Using the things those early bikes taught them, they have moved on to something better, something more their age.

The reason some people and churches don't grow is because they're still on training wheels. Whether it's security or simplicity, or the fear of something bigger that keeps them there, it matters little. We never move faster than we are equipped to move.

This is what the Hebrew writer was talking about when he said,

> Therefore leaving the elementary teachings about the Christ, let us press on to maturity, not laying again a foundation of repentance from dead works and of faith toward God, of instruction about washings, and laying on of hands, and the resurrection of the dead, and eternal judgment. (Hebrews 6:1,2)

He was not saying that these were worthless doctrines, but they are things that must be built on as we move on to bigger concepts. We must press on to maturity, and that can't happen when we refuse to learn, question and grow. We can peddle around indefinitely on training wheels, but we will miss the real joy of cruising with Christ up the higher hills. Proper equipping allows us to soar to new heights, conquer mountains, and fly through the valleys of life. You can't do that on training wheels.

The smug attitude that proclaims "I've arrived" doesn't want to hear about equipping. Equipping assumes that there are deficiencies, and those who already have all the answers can't accept that. Truth has become a syllogistic conclusion instead of a growing process. Once you have the interpretive methodology worked out, faith becomes an equation and church a place to check your answers. Growing in Christ is no longer a matter of love, but logic. That doesn't mean there is no place for logic in our faith, but Paul declared all actions meaningless, both mental and physical, if those actions do not have love (1 Corinthians 13).

Equipping involves the recognition that we are spiritual street people who have been cleansed, clothed and covered by a loving God who should have destroyed us. Such action of God is called grace, and we have been called to grow in both grace and knowledge. That's where equipping comes in.

DISCUSSION QUESTIONS

1. How do Christians praise God?
2. Is attending the assembly something we do for God?

3. How much equipping takes place in your assemblies?

4. Is it possible to grow spiritually without being equipped to grow?

5. What is implied about us if we feel no need for equipping?

CHAPTER TEN
Pass The Ammunition

A wonderful discourse on Christian togetherness is found in Ephesians 4. A simple working (not to mention preaching) outline of the chapter is

Uniting in Christ (v. 1-10)
Growing in Christ (v. 11-16)
Living in Christ (v. 17-32)

Because I am using "equipping" as synonymous with "growing," let's examine verses 11-16. The passage is a mouthful of meat that can be better digested when seen as three bites.

EQUIPPERS

The first bite covers equippers. "And He gave some as apostles, and some as prophets, and some as evangelists, and some as pastors and teachers" (v. 11). God determined that these leaders are the primary equippers of the church. Without stopping to deal with modern day prophets and Latter Day apostles, let's just say that elders, preachers and teachers are the front-line trainers for Christ. Their job is to lead, feed, guide, instruct, disciple, push-pull, hug, lug, bug and, generally speaking, raise.

This job description is not for everybody. Paul emphatically and repeatedly says that only "some" were given the task to equip. These are people with experience, spiritual depth, and a desire to serve. They are "How can I help you?" folks who get their kicks watching babes in Christ become hardened vets in His army. They wouldn't dream of allowing a new recruit to go off to war without making him aware of all the gear and resources available to assist him. And then they show him how to use those resources. That's important, because an equipper shows and tells.

All the details of driving a stick-shift car were explained to me several times before I sat in the driver's seat. Those instructions never took; they hit my brain like a flat rock hits water. But when someone sat next to me and showed me how to use the clutch and gearshift, I never forgot. Sermons, lectures and discourses have a place in equipping, but those speeches must be coupled with practical training. I have adapted an old proverb: *Preach a sermon and give a man a meal, but show him how to grow spiri-*

tually and you give him a meal ticket for life. Why can't the assembly be, among other things, a "show and tell" experience?

Thank God for church leaders who take seriously their responsibility to equip. People in churches are crying for preachers to step down from their pulpits and show them how to cope with life's storms. *Churches are inwardly pleading with their elders to walk away from their conference tables and come to their dinner table and feed the flock.* Teachers need to set down their chalk, drop down on their knees, and show those little ones how to pray.

Leaders must look to Jesus. He spent three and a half years showing His apostles what He wanted. When He said "Love," He had loved. When He said, "Care," He had cared. When He said, "Carry a cross," He showed them how. When He said, "Go," He had gone.

EQUIPPING

The second bite describes equipping.

> . . . for the equipping of the saints for the work of service, to the building up of the body of Christ; until we all attain to the unity of the faith, and of the knowledge of the Son of God, to the mature man, to the measure of the stature which belongs to the fullness of Christ. (v. 12,13)

When the drill instructor first sets his eyes on the young, insecure boy on his first day at boot camp, the DI knows exactly what he wants that boy to become when he is through with him. If he has done his job as a drill instructor, the boy should become a capable, dependable soldier.

What are the church's Equippers supposed to be equipping saints to do? Paul said that saints should be equipped to do "the work of service." Our list would be very different from Paul's. We would have placed "learn what to do in the assembly" at the top of our list. We have a twofold approach to Christianity. First, one must become a Christian; second, one must go to church. Paul says to teach the saints how to serve. "Well, if a person will go to church, then he will learn how to serve," someone responds. Since when has that been the case? Maybe we've had the chariot before the horse. If someone learns to serve, then that person will learn the value of the assembly?

People always have had difficulty understanding New Testament service. It's unnatural to want to serve instead of being served. It's unnatural to seek to be the last or least or, for that matter, to do things in secret. Yet, when we took up our cross to follow Jesus, where did we think He would lead us? To the plush and padded pew or to a serving line where we dispense bread and fish? To a mahogany table inscribed with one of His sayings or to a towel and washbasin and a row of dirty feet?

I wouldn't want to build a case on whether or not Paul listed these elements of equipping in order of priority, but it is significant that the first thing elders, preachers and teachers should equip saints to do is serve. If a church is not a serving church, whose fault is it? If the level of serving has been going down, what does that say about the church leaders? Have the elders, preachers and teachers forgotten that their jobs are serving jobs? Is more petty power playing and recognition grabbing going on than unselfish giving and humble leading? Are elders so busy making decisions, balancing budgets and attending meetings that they can't show saints how to serve? Are ministers so wrung out by meeting everyone's expectations that they don't have time to equip servants? Have our teachers become religious theoreticians rather than practical, relevant equippers?

Church leaders exist for the purpose of equipping saints to serve. Sure they have other responsibilities, but none are stated more clearly anywhere in the Bible. When did the New Testament church leaders do their equipping of the saints? Equipping took place when they assembled together and when they met in small groups. This idea will be dealt with later, but how much equipping takes place in your assemblies?

Next Paul said equippers were there for " . . . building up the body of Christ." When Christians come together, the leaders have the responsibility to equip them with what they need to grow as a church. This growth is to be in both Spirit and size. "Equip for growth?" someone asks. Absolutely. We have always seen church growth as something you pray for, hire, or draw from other congregations. At best, if growth happens it is an accident and not because we trained, planned and caused it.

Don't confuse equipping and encouraging. They go together and depend on each other. They are the ball and bat in the softball game, you can't play without both. But just being encouraged by what happens in your assembly doesn't mean that you have been equipped to grow. People have been going to church for years and have been uplifted, but the church isn't any stronger or bigger because of the experience.

Encouragement is the grease that keeps the equipment working. We've been blowing steam without having it hooked up to an engine because we've left off equipping.

In this Ephesians passage, Paul is talking about the need for equipping in order to bring about spiritual and numerical growth. Such growth is God's plan. He wants church leaders to enable saints to grow. This is about as clear-cut a command as you will find anywhere in the Bible. So when and where does it take place?

God gives us a time limit on equipping: " . . . until we all attain to the unity of the faith, and of the knowledge of the Son of God." We've got to keep it up until we have unity of faith and knowledge. Maybe that explains why some leaders don't equip anyone anymore. They think we already have reached that point of unity. Or maybe they are just surrounded by folks who agree on all the doctrinal issues, so everyone assumes the group has unity.

I desperately wanted to be in on the things my older brother did with his friends. I followed them like a stray dog which infuriated them. They ran from me, threatened me, and even locked me out of my own house as they tried to keep their group free from the unwanted, too young, and smart-mouthed little brother. I was only four years younger, but that was enough to mark me as an outsider. They only wanted kids their own age to be part of their group.

Many times in the church we have acted that same way. Before you can be part of our group, you must have the right answers, the right interpretations, the right doctrine, the right knowledge, the right traditions, the right clothing, and even the right translation of the Bible. It's OK to be a babe in Christ as long as you are full grown. Faith and knowledge must already be attained before we extend fellowship and unity. Somehow, we have forgotten that spiritual growth is a process, and we have made it a prerequisite. We have been so busy drawing lines of fellowship, erecting walls, and closing doors that we haven't had time to equip the saints for unity.

Everyone is at different levels of knowledge and faith in Jesus. Equippers say, "Come, let's grow together." Unity will develop as we draw closer to each other and as our faith and knowledge of Him increases. Unity is illusive because usually it is not based on faith and knowledge of Jesus. He is the rallying point, the hub, the King, and the Super Glue that holds us all together.

Equippers help folks get to the "mature man" point (v. 13). They don't expect them to be there because then the leaders become obsolete. After all, we are all priests with our own direct access to God. We just need to be equipped to enable us to function in the priesthood. Isn't the greatest goal of any leader in the church to help brethren learn to depend on God? In essence, shouldn't leaders want to work themselves right out of their job, to put themselves in a position where all they need to do is love and encourage a saint who is spiritually grown up?

Because Paul was an apostle, he was an equipper. His writings are replete with analogies comparing spiritual growth to physical growth. He talked about Christians being babes, immature, children, and other stages right to adulthood. He viewed his job as being a spiritual father with children to raise. He said,

> And we proclaim Him, admonishing every man and teaching every man with all wisdom, that we may present every man complete in Christ. (Colossians 1:28)

Complete, or perfected, means that they, spiritually speaking, got their acts together. Jesus is in control of their lives.

Much joy comes in leading someone to Christ. Knowing that you have picked the Devil's pocket and helped save a soul from hell is a real kick. But, an equally thrilling feeling is seeing one you have been equipping grow to maturity and become an equipper himself. *Watching a brother or sister grow in love, display a Christlike attitude when dealing with others, and start taking others under their wings to protect and guide them are among the most satisfying sights a church leader could see.*

> . . . to the measure of the stature which belongs to the fullness of Christ" means that the end product of equipping is Christians who are Christlike. (v. 13)

Two decades have passed since I first read the story in high school English literature class, but I still remember it. The story is Nathaniel Hawthorne's *The Great Stone Face*. The Great Stone Face was a mountainside that had the face of a man on it, a face carved by nature and admired by all. A little boy named Ernest was especially attracted to the image on the mountain. A prophecy said that the face on the mountain belonged to some great man who was yet to come along. To Ernest the face became the symbol of dignity and kindness, and – without intending to be idolatrous – to Ernest it looked like the face of God. Ernest spent his growing years looking for the man whose face was sculpted on the mountainside. He suspected several "great men" might be candidates, but each time, after closer inspection, he decided against them. The face wasn't the wealthy Mr. Gathergold, or the war hero General Blood-and-Thunder, or Old Stony Phiz the politician. Surprisingly, the face immortalized on the mountainside wasn't even Rev. Dr. Battleblast's face.

As the years went by, Ernest gained a reputation as a kind and loving man. One day, after several others had suggested it, he realized that the face on the mountainside was his. Was it all a coincidence? Had the Great Stone Face been a premonition of what he would become? Or was he influenced by the object of his life's attention?

As we keep Jesus in our hearts and before our eyes, we are transformed into His likeness (2 Corinthians 3:18). Our transformation doesn't happen overnight. One just comes to the understanding one day, after a lifetime of looking at Him, that the face on the cross is his.

EQUIPPED

The last bite describes what will happen to those equipped.

As a result, we are no longer to be children, tossed here and there by waves, and carried about by every wind of doctrine, by the trickery of men, by craftiness in deceitful scheming; but speaking the truth in love, we are to grow up in all aspects into him, who is the head, even Christ, from whom the whole body, being fitted and held together by that which every joint supplies, according to the proper working of each individual part, causes the growth of the body for the building up of itself in love. (Ephesians 4:14-16)

If those called by God to be equippers have done their duty, Paul says results will come. Those equipped will have a foundation and a force, both of which are just two different ways of viewing Jesus. This passage of Scripture firmly established the centrality of Christ in the lives of Christians and the church.

Paul gave the church at Corinth this identical message. Remember the paradox of 1 Corinthians 15:58? Paul said,

Therefore, my beloved brethren, be steadfast, immovable, always abounding in the work of the Lord, knowing that your toil is not in vain in the Lord.

To be "immovable" and "abounding" at the same time makes no sense at all unless you understand how central Jesus is to this formula. Christians are cemented in the Word of God and are compelled by the Son of God. They remain immovable in their convictions. Jesus Christ is their convictions. Jesus, therefore, is both the foundation for steadfastness and the force behind the toil. Without Him all would be empty, meaningless or, as Paul said, vain.

When equippers have been equipping, those equipped have their foundation in Christ and their force, or power, from Christ. Paul gave us a description of each of these results.

When Christians have a firm foundation in Jesus Christ they stop being children. They have matured to the point that they no longer talk in terms of "my," "mine," and "me." Selfishness and pettiness have been outgrown like a pair of old tennis shoes, which are too ugly to be hand-me-downs. Life is more than eating dessert, getting new toys, and throwing temper tantrums. Giving has replaced getting on their wish list, and "Do I have to?" has been replaced by "When can I?" More important, "I can do it myself" has changed to "I can do all things through Christ."

With Jesus as their foundation, Christians are no longer unstable. They are anchors in solid ground instead of rubber duckies that float along wherever the current or the wind takes them. They are part of a team. They have their feet firmly planted and their shoulders squared, ready to meet the advancing enemy. They have fellow fighters on either side of them, and a large contingent of cheerleaders are yelling, "Hold that line!"

Finally, Christians who have their foundation in Jesus are no longer naive. They are no longer suckered by spiritual sleight of hand or holy hocus-pocus. They are impressed by the Master and not by men who use, abuse and confuse the masses into joining a serfdom instead of the kingdom. They are experienced, battle-hardened soldiers who know a snow-job when they see one.

Evidently the Christians at Corinth were still naive when Paul wrote 2 Corinthians. They were being tricked into following some false apostles and were even being abused by them. (See 2 Corinthians 10-12.)

111

Maybe that is why Paul closed his letter by asking the Corinthian Christians to examine themselves to see if Jesus was in them (13:5). When we are finally connected to the Vine, we have the strength we need to fight off the parasites.

FIREPOWER

One of the darkest hours of English military history provides us with a good example for the church. In 1879 the British sent a large army into the Zululand to protect their interests in South Africa. As the main army moved deeper into Zulu territory, a rear guard contingent of 1,700 men was left behind at a jagged mountain named Isandhlwana. Within hours after being left by the main army, the detachment was attacked by 20,000 Zulu warriors, who were armed with primitive spears and clubs. Despite the devastating toll they inflicted on the Zulus with their rifle and cannon fire, the British fighters were overwhelmed and decimated within two hours. The primary reason for their defeat was the commander's failure to keep his soldiers in a tight fighting group and concentrate his firepower.

That night, just a few miles away from Isandhlwana, the heroic battle of Rorke's Drift took place. Rorke's Drift was defended by about 100 men, who had to cover a 400-yard walled perimeter that connected a storehouse, a hospital and a corral. They had an inner wall to pull back to as they tightened their defenses.

At 5:30 p.m. they were attacked by 4,000 experienced Zulus. The battle that followed has gone down in history as one of the great last-stand battles of all time. For ten hours the fighting raged. Under superior leadership the defenders were organized, effective and unwavering as they fought off charge after charge. By 4 a.m. the next day the Zulus withdrew. At 7 a.m. they were seen heading for home. The defenders had fired 20,000 rounds of ammunition. Fifteen men had died; two were dying; seven were badly wounded; and nearly everyone had minor injuries. There were more Victoria Crosses given for the battle at Rorke's Drift than for any other single action in British history.

At Isandhlwana, the British soldiers were outnumbered ten to one and were overwhelmed in two hours. At Rorke's Drift, where they were facing odds of forty to one, they held their ground successfully for more than ten hours. Much can be said for drawing in defenses and concentrating power.[23]

There is no telling what Christians could accomplish if we would learn to draw closer together and concentrate our power. We find it much easier to stand tall and hold our ground when someone stands with us. If all of us who are firmly grounded in Jesus Christ unite the power He has given us, no army of Satan could stand against us. But we must have both the right foundation and the right force, and the assembly is a perfect place to develop both.

Just as our foundation is Christ, so our force or power is Christ. Our power comes from Him in the form of unity, dependency and love (Ephesians 4:15,16). Christ is the Head, and we are His body. We grow in all aspects because of Him. He holds us together; He supplies every need; and He causes us to grow. He is the "power that works within us" (Ephesians 3:20).

Love is our secret weapon. Paul said that we speak

in love and grow in love. To attempt to grow without a loving spirit is to try swimming without water; you go through the motions but you don't get anywhere. Love is a powerful force that was meant to be used in high concentrations. When we pool our love, we cause more chain reactions than a nuclear bomb. So why isn't a huge reaction happening? People aren't being equipped to make it happen.

DISCUSSION QUESTIONS

1. What does Ephesians 4 have to say about equipping? Is it optional?
2. How should elders equip the saints?
3. Is the assembly an appropriate place to learn "how" to serve and not just "why" to serve?
4. How does encouragement interface with equipping?
5. What does equipping have to do with unity?

CHAPTER ELEVEN
Regrouped And Refitted

Let's take a sentimental journey through the eyes of Graham Kendrick from his book *Learning to Worship As a Way of Life*.

I can well remember in my own childhood how going to church seemed so often to be little more than a lesson in patience and endurance. I longed for 'the service' to come to an end. I would watch the dust floating in the shafts of summer sunlight, or scratch with my 'collection penny' in the varnish of the pew in front of me. The trouble was, nothing ever happened; well, certain prescribed things did, but nothing unexpected or unusual – unless somebody fainted, or had a fit, or knocked over a pile of hymn books.[24]

This passage is more than a childhood memory for many. It could be a description of last Sunday for some adults. In fact, it's been so long since folks found their assembly to be a positive, growing experience that our first reaction to something different is to label it liberal.

Ephesians 4:11-16 clearly lays out a plan of action for spiritual growth. Church leaders are to equip the church with specific things, which will bring about specific results. Now, when and where does equipping take place? Equipping happens whenever Christians get together.

Chapter 1 explained what the purpose of assembly is – togetherness. Christians assemble to be together. We don't assemble to worship because that's what our lives are. We don't assemble to perform rituals because no rituals are found in the New Testament, just togetherness builders. One of the main reasons Christians assemble is to be equipped.

"Wait a second," someone protests. "It sounds to me like you are talking about what takes place in the Bible class, not the formal assembly." Where in the New Testament have you ever found a distinction in the church's assemblies? Did the early church have Bible classes and formal assemblies? The only thing we read in the Bible about Christian assemblies is that they had them and that they were told to equip one another for spiritual growth. We have no biblical authority for formalism in our assemblies. We do have a need and a command to be together. Togetherness should meet the need we have for encouraging and equipping in order for us to grow into Christ's likeness.

We have gone so far down the road of traditionalism that we can't see how equipping fits into our assembly. People are bored to death, yet they need to be equipped for life. Unless we happen to pick up a morsel of training from the sermon, our assemblies are usually void of any equipping. Should we be surprised with the lack of spiritual and numerical growth that characterizes most churches today?

The assembly should be an equipping experience. *All the things we are told to do when we assemble together are tools for encouragement and equipping.* Elders, preachers and teachers are, as Paul said, equippers. Teaching and preaching are not religious monologues on theology. They are to be "training in righteousness" that deals in terms of practical application. When Paul spoke until midnight in Acts 20, what was he doing? Was it a discourse or a "How To" course? Was he training or just talking? Jesus' command to "teach them to observe" is tantamount to "show them how to do it."

HEAVY EQUIPMENT IN USE

What have we missed because of our failure to use communion as an equipping experience? A time when all eyes should be intently focused on Jesus is a wonderful time to learn more about imitating Him. As we rejoice in our common salvation together, we need to be helping each other draw closer to Him. Sure, we need to meditate and examine ourselves, but the Holy Spirit called it *koinonia*, not isolation time.

When we sing, we teach and admonish one another, but we also fill our hearts with melodic messages of love, commitment, and a hundred other con-

117

cepts that beg to be internalized. How many lives have been turned around by a simple challenge to "Count your blessings, name them one by one" or to "Work for the night is coming"?

In our climb to be Christlike, learning that it is more blessed to give than to receive is a Mount Everest. The opportunity to give as we prosper on the first day of the week keeps us climbing up that mountain. We should be learning to share, care and bear as we become cheerful givers. If contribution is just a ritual passing of the plates, we lose a tremendous chance to equip one another.

One of the most beautiful examples of equipping is seen in the way Jesus taught His apostles to pray. He taught them what prayer was. Then He said, "And when you pray, pray like this." He showed them how to pray. He taught them to not pray like the Pharisees, but to be humble.

In prayer we communicate with God together. Prayer is a great unifying act, and it is a Christlike act. Can prayer be a tool to equip us? If not, why do it together?

The question that should be on the lips of every Christian is "How can we maximize the opportunities for equipping in our assemblies?" The Lord wants us to grow. We want to grow. Why not do what He wants us to do to cause growth? Training, or equipping, is not an extra or secondary activity, and it shouldn't play second fiddle to anything else we do in our assembly. Equipping is not an elective for the church, it is part of our major. Christians don't come together to get their tickets punched, but to have their needs met. We must discover what the needs of the church are and then equip folks to handle those needs.

The assembly can and must meet needs if it is going to be an effective, spiritually enriching experience. Unfortunately, "needs" is a dirty word in some circles today. If a congregation is truly trying to be "needs oriented," it is promptly called a worldly church. Some assume that meeting needs means that a church is being self-centered and man oriented instead of God-centered and Christ oriented. Why? Is God not glorified and praised when Christians reach out in love and heal one another's hurts? Why is it being self-centered to equip people to have happier homes, healthier self-esteem and better relationships?

Folks come to the assembly emotionally and spiritually rung-out and in need of guidance. We respond by telling them to sit quietly and concentrate on the "acts of worship, and that will take care of you." Do we not realize that the assembly, maybe more than any other place in our lives, is the one place where we try to look our best and hide our problems?

Everyone is always shocked to find out, after it's too late, that the Joneses are separated and the Smiths are having serious problems with their son. After all, they were at every assembly, smiled at everybody, shook hands warmly, and looked like the perfect families.

Is it being self-centered to have relevant sermons, relaxed surroundings, and plenty of personal interaction to discover if anyone needs help? Time has come for us to realize that the very structure of our assemblies inhibits and discourages helping people while it encourages religious facades.

People are crying for equipping, and we tell them, "Sorry, but you come to church to give, not to get." Again, where are the scriptures to justify such assertions? The assembly may not be the best place to deal with benevolence, counseling and physical needs. But are we not being God-centered when we consider and meet the spiritual and emotional needs of our church family? Is "bear one another's burdens" a non-assembly activity? When do we "not merely look out for your own personal interests, but also for the interests of others"? Is it out of place to "rejoice with those who rejoice, and weep with those who weep" in the assembly? Do we "encourage the fainthearted, help the weak" only in the foyer?

The assembly is not the only place, or even the best place to meet all the needs of those gathered together, but to say that being "needs oriented" is "too man-centered" is to misunderstand how God wants us to show our love for Him. Redemption is the greatest salve for an aching heart, but the assembly is primarily for the redeemed. Those assembled are people who have waited all week for a sympathetic ear, a kind smile, and a caring family. Equipping must include meeting needs, or we will just be "feeding hay to a dead horse." The greater danger, however, is that we may be guilty of closing our hearts to brothers in need, and thus bringing into question our love for God (1 John 3:17).

EFFECTIVELY EQUIPPED

The young lad was appalled that anyone would dare taunt the armies of the living God. Relatives and spectators assumed the young kid was some smart aleck just trying to goad them into an unwinnable fight with the Philistine giant. When the king heard about the boy's willingness to stand up to the loud-mouthed monstrosity who shamed Israel, he told the boy, "Go, and may the Lord be with you." Then in an effort to ensure victory, the king equipped David with his own armor, which was the best money could buy. The armor was shiny, thick and oppressively heavy. Lending the suit was a neat idea, only David couldn't walk in it, and he had no idea how to use it. A brave champion almost went into battle with the wrong equipment. With God's help and using the right equipment, defeating Goliath was a piece of cake for David.

Many great soldiers have been struck down in the battle of life because they were improperly equipped. We keep trying to put Saul's armor on people who need to learn how to use a sling. Using Saul's armor was typical, traditional thinking. What was needed was trust in God and a willingness to use unorthodox equipment.

DISCUSSION QUESTIONS

1. Why is it assumed that equipping belongs in the Bible class and not in the assembly?

2. Are the assembly activities "acts of worship" or tools for togetherness? On what scriptures do you base your answer?

3. How can the communion be an equipping experience? How can singing, praying, giving and preaching be equipping experiences?

4. What are some of the ways Jesus equipped His apostles?

5. What happens to Christians who are not properly equipped?

SECTION FOUR
ENJOYMENT
AND THE ASSEMBLY

CHAPTER TWELVE
The Cheerless Church

Peter and John were on their way to prayer meeting. They were an ordinary looking couple of guys with an extraordinary love for God. They had made this trip so many times in their lives that they could have made it blindfolded. Dodging carts, horses, livestock, and thousands of busy townfolks, they made their way to one of the busiest entrances of the temple, the gate called Beautiful.

One of the many street people who clogged up the entrance of the gate was a crippled man. This man had been handicapped from birth and therefore was reduced to begging for a living. No one hired handicapped people because it was assumed that their condition was the result of sin in their lives. Each day this man was carried to the gate and forced to rely on handouts from the few who acknowledged his presence. More than likely, Peter and John had seen him there many times. We don't know if they had ever given the poor man money; they were poor themselves. Maybe, like most everyone else, they had ignored the man. This time, however, Peter and John had an offer too good for the man to refuse.

Before he could hit them with his sales pitch, Peter told him they were fresh out of dough but rich in the power of Jesus Christ. "Walk," said Peter as he grabbed the guy by the hand and helped him to his feet. Because the man had never been on his feet before, he knew at once that he had been healed. He was released by Peter and he stood on his own seeing the world from a standing position for the first time in his life.

With his arms spread wide for balance, he took his first step. So complete was the miracle that he began to walk with no problems at all. He spun around and was amazed at his own stability. Then "he entered the temple with them, walking and leaping and praising God. And all the people saw him walking and praising God" (Acts 3:1-9).

Each week millions who have been healed by God meet together to celebrate their wholeness. They have been freed from the shackles of sin and are no longer handicapped by sin's destructive power. They have been touched by the Great Physician, who gave them what He had to give, something far better than silver and gold. Why then does their celebration look more like the beggar before he met Peter and John than after he met them? Why are they sitting, handicapped and begging when they should be walking, leaping

126

and praising God?

Is our response to God not determined by the value we place in what He has done for us? The lame man didn't have to be told to praise God. He was so thrilled to be healed that praising God was the natural thing to do. He was happy about what God had done, so he leaped and shouted praises to His name.

This presents us with two questions. First, are we truly thankful for God's grace and glad that it has been given to us? Second, do we act like we are thankful and glad?

I had been a Christian for several years before I discovered that we are supposed to be happy. I was young and not thrilled with this "going to church" business. *Everyone at church seemed to be in pain. Faces were stern, serious and severe. Laughter in the assembly was unheard of; fun was out of the question; and informality was anathema.*

Even as a youngster I realized that happiness was a state of mind. Enough folks smiled and laughed outside the church building for me to conclude that the facade of sadness was necessary in order to be seen as spiritually mature by everyone else. Still, I just knew it must be written somewhere in the Bible that people were not supposed to enjoy church. I couldn't find where it was written, but I was certain the passage was something akin to "No pain, no gain."

REMORSEFUL RELIGION

I can't help but wonder where the cheerless church came from. It is not the church of the New Testament. Does it have its roots in the woeful cathedrals of the

Dark Ages? Is it a holdover from early American Puritanism? Or do we just believe that we are being more spiritual if we act downcast about an upbeat Lord?

Writing about the assembly in his wonderful book, *The Pharisee's Guide to Total Holiness*, William Coleman said, "Maybe they have become exercises in penitence to be endured as punishments from God. Possibly we revel in their dullness, because it speaks well of our piety that we did not enjoy the experience."[25]

Most of this is due to a basic misunderstanding of the purpose of the assembly. The assembly is not an exercise in toughness but togetherness. If this statement is correct, it brings us to an interesting question. Did God intend for Christians to enjoy togetherness? Remember that I am using "togetherness" as synonymous with the "assembly."

One could easily become trite at this point and say "A truly spiritually mature person will enjoy the assembly no matter what happens." In theory that's true, but then around our house the tooth fairy is a theory too. Do we enjoy the assembly in spite of what happens or because of what happens? Did the early church enjoy their assemblies and look forward to them, or did those Christians view them as merely an obligation?

Because we are asking lots of questions, let's get personal with a question. What do you consistently enjoy most about your assemblies? We all like the singing – when it is good. We all like the sermons – when they are good. But, what if the singing and the sermons are bad or uninspiring? Are enjoyment and enrichment hit-and-miss propositions? When you really think it through completely, you discover that consistent joy comes from being with people you love – Togetherness – *Koinonia.*

When people start talking about their most meaningful and enjoyable assemblies, they invariably will mention retreats, devotionals, fellowships, classes and prayer groups. The reason for this is that the informal nature of these assemblies allows for more relationship building, intimacy and togetherness.

Donald Babner and Sarah Ricketts combined their talents and wrote a beautiful little study book titled *Building People Through a Caring Sharing Fellowship.* In a chapter about *"Koinonia* – The Real Thing," they write:

> I believe that when we experience the forgiveness and love of God and extend it to one another, we are actually foretasting a little bit of heaven. We are told that heaven is a real place and the New Jerusalem will have streets of gold and pearly gates. But I think heaven is more than a place. I believe the essence of it is koinonia, an ever-widening relationship with God and one another. I can get tired of sight-seeing, but I never get tired of growing relationships. I've heard people say, in response to real koinonia, "If it can be like this on earth, what is it going to be like in heaven?"[26]

When people have the opportunity to grow in love, the assembly can be heaven on earth. We enjoy being together, growing together and working together. That not only means consistent joy, but consistent attendance. Anything else is sight-seeing, and we all get tired of that.

Isn't it wonderful to know that our God "richly supplies us with all things to enjoy" (1 Timothy 6:17)? He gave us life, His Son's life, and eternal life. Peter said that we have been given all things "pertaining to life and godliness" (2 Peter 1:3). As a result we "greatly rejoice with joy inexpressible and full of glory" (1 Pet. 1:8).

The answer to the question, "Did God intend for Christians to enjoy the assembly?" is yes, a thousand times yes. Jesus proclaimed, "The Sabbath was made for man, and not man for the Sabbath" (Mark 2:27). He was talking about the Old Law, but the principle is the same. The assembly was made for man, not man for the assembly. Our coming together is intended to be an enjoyable experience as a result of the encouragement and equipping every participant received.

DISCUSSION QUESTIONS

1. What is a good, biblical definition of New Testament joy?

2. Can your assembly be described as joyful?

3. What do you enjoy most about your assembly? Why?

4. Is it being self-centered to expect the assembly to be joyful and uplifting?

5. Did God intend for us to enjoy the assembly? How do you know?

CHAPTER THIRTEEN
Delicious Doctrines

A great deal is being said these days about the importance of a balanced diet. Researchers are just beginning to realize how many diseases and illnesses can be avoided if we will eat balanced portions from the five major food groups. I know all this and more because I am married to a registered dietician. So I make a valiant effort to eat those things my taste buds tell me are inedible. Having kids around has made it harder to follow my old motto, which states, "If it's green or healthy, don't eat it." Nevertheless, I eat things that are good for me because I know I should. Usually I eat them quickly and in as few bites as good manners will allow. Then I slowly relish the juicy, fattening, swimming in butter, artery clogging things I really like. A vegetable is a vegetable, but a hot, succulent steak is a *chef d'oeurve*, a masterpiece.

I don't dwell on foods I don't care for. I don't skip or avoid them. I just make sure I get what I need, and then I move on to the main course, to those delicious things that dreams are made of. The choice is mine. I can chose to spend my time on a side dish, or I can savor the entree.

In the church, we sometimes poke around in the side dishes of God's great feast, and we have left virtually no room for the *piece de resistance*. What happened to spiritually well-balanced meals? God has served us some healthy portions of delightful doctrines such as happiness, rejoicing, praising and thanksgiving. Yet we dwell on differences, issues, social ills and personal shortcomings. Should we skip or avoid these things? Of course not, but they are side dishes that we need to eat on the way to the main dish.

The sheer magnitude of what the Bible has to say about enjoyable dishes like happiness (or blessedness), rejoicing, praising and thanksgiving should be enough to prove my point. Although we should never decide any biblical point based on numbers of verses, we should find it significant to realize that these concepts are dominant throughout the Bible. In fact, they absolutely dwarf the few passages that discuss the assembly. These "main course" concepts are blended together with enjoyment and served in the assembly.

HAPPINESS

Volumes have been written about the Sermon on

132

the Mount. One could spend a lifetime delving into its richness and depth. One also could dissect it so much that he might miss the whole point of Jesus' message. The Beatitudes are an excellent example of teachings that are both deep and simple. Although Jesus says so many great things, the basic principle is that if your heart is right, God will take care of you and you will be happy.

Because this begins in the heart, we can be happy even when persecuted. In fact, Jesus said, "Rejoice and be glad" if that happens, because we will be greatly rewarded by our Father. So happiness is not contingent on the conditions of life, but the condition of our heart. *It stands to reason that if happy-hearted people get together, they will enhance one another's happiness.*

REJOICING

Heartfelt happiness leads to rejoicing. Nothing is more pitiful than mechanical rejoicing. I am not referring to instruments but rather structure. Is rejoicing a matter of singing a song, or maybe a song with a fast beat? Is it something we can schedule at specific times and say, "Let's all rejoice now"? What is rejoicing if it is not the result of spontaneous joy? Are we really rejoicing if it doesn't come from our hearts?

In the Beatitudes when Jesus referred to being persecuted for righteousness' sake, Luke records Jesus as saying, "Be glad in that day, and leap for joy, for behold, your reward is great in heaven" (Luke 6:23). Leaping for joy? That's right, but don't do it where any church people will see you. That's way too emotional

133

and dangerously close to being holy rollers. It is certainly unbecoming for a serious and established churchgoer. Leap for joy, and get labeled for life.

Nothing is more biblical than rejoicing. The New Testament is replete with commands about and examples of rejoicing. The early Christians were quick to rejoice and constantly were reminding each other of its importance. It seems that they looked for excuses to rejoice, and if there was no particular event about which to rejoice, they simply rejoiced in their relationship with God and each other.

According to *Vine's Expository Dictionary of New Testament Words*, five primary words are used in the New Testament for rejoicing. *Chairo* was used when there was a special occasion for rejoicing (such as upon hearing the Gospel (Acts 13:48) in salvation (Acts 8:39) over liberty in Christ (Acts 15:31) over hope (Romans 12:12) in the Lord. *Sunchairo* is used of rejoicing in suffering (Philippians 2:17,18), in honor of fellow believers (1 Corinthians 12:26), and in triumph of truth (1 Corinthians 13:6). A superlative form of the word that referred to rejoicing greatly was *agalliao*, which was used in conjunction with faith in God (1 Peter 1:8) and salvation (Acts 16:34). Another form of the word is *euphraino*, which denoted to cheer, gladden or make merry (Acts 2:26; Romans 15:10). *Kauchaomai* carried the connotation of boasting or to glory in (as in the hope of glory of God (Romans 5:2) and in Christ Jesus (Philippians 3:3).[27]

Enough sermon material is here to preach for years about nothing but rejoicing. Certainly it is safe to say that God's people are heavily into rejoicing. We rejoice in our hearts, our homes and our assemblies. Rejoice is just joy with a reason. We have joy in our

134

assemblies because of the love we have for God and one another. We are happy to be together, and we rejoice in the Lordship of Jesus Christ.

How do we put joy in our assemblies? Joy is more a matter of attitude than actions. You can't stand up next Sunday and declare that from now on everyone is going to enjoy the assembly. You have to make it enjoyable. Let people share and express love for each other. Be happy about being Christians. Meet needs, not schedules. Touch hearts, hold hands, and wash feet. Appreciate one another. Thank God for His guidance. Relax and enjoy your togetherness.

What is the primary way in our culture that we show appreciation publicly? Applause. It says to the recipients, "We truly appreciate what you have done, and we want to publicly recognize you and honor you." Because Christians are into rejoicing and showing appreciation, how could it possibly be out of place to applaud in the assembly? I am not talking about raucous cheers and shouting, but sincere appreciation that is displayed naturally by uninhibited applause.

We certainly are not guilty of overdoing the showing of appreciation. I believe we will be held accountable by God for all the missed opportunities we have had to show appreciation. I would rather err on the side of overdoing it than on the side of negligence. "The problem with applause in the assembly," declares the threatened theologian, "is that it is man-centered and not God-centered." Doesn't the same argument apply to the "holy kiss"? That must be the reason we don't do it any more. Is it man-centered for God's people to show appreciation to God's people with godly motivation in their hearts and to the glory of God? Jesus settled that argument long ago. He said

135

that love given to the "least of these" is love given to Him (Matthew 25:40). It no longer is man-centered when it is done in the name of Jesus.

I had been talking to my congregation about this for some time, and they were starting to feel somewhat comfortable with applauding someone who was baptized, recognized, or in some way in need of public encouragement. They would applaud if I started it or asked them to. It's difficult to break out of the formalism we have known all our lives.

A special member of our congregation was a young man named Rob. Rob was in his mid-30's and had been born with the debilitating disease of cerebral palsy. Rob couldn't talk, walk, or do most of the things we all take for granted. He was a very loving man with loving parents who cared for him, but most important, Rob was a Christian. We all loved him dearly, and we always made a point of talking to him because his mind was as good as any of ours. He understood us completely, but he couldn't say anything understandable to us.

Through the miracle of modern technology, a computer was made that would allow people like Rob to talk through the computer. Rob and his family wanted one, but the computers were very expensive and buying one would strain the family's resources terribly. So we took up a special contribution at church and bought one for him. The difficult part for us all was waiting for it to arrive.

Then one Sunday evening Rob came into the church building with an unusual little box on the front of his wheelchair. We knew it was the computer, but Rob didn't demonstrate it for anyone. During the closing announcements and just before the dismissal, it was announced that Rob had something he wanted to say. The room was packed, but we could have heard a church mouse walking on the carpet. Rob had never been able to clearly communicate in his entire life, so we all held our breath. Rob was in his wheelchair in the middle aisle, in the center of the auditorium. He strained and jerked his pointer finger around, and it came to rest in the computer. Then a mechanical voice said, "My name is Rob. Thank you for my computer."

I stood at the rear of the auditorium absolutely amazed at what I'd heard from Rob. Then all at once the entire audience erupted with thunderous applause, spontaneous applause. I was glad I was in the back. I felt a little embarrassed about the tears that rolled down my face. Those tears were tears of joy for Rob and tears of rejoicing that my brethren were not afraid to show what was on their hearts.

If Rob's computer had spoken a few years earlier, we'd have sat there like a bunch of corpses wanting to do something to express our joy but afraid of "what others might think."

PRAISE AND THANKSGIVING

What does praise have to do with enjoyment? Nothing or everything, depending on how you understand praise. If praise is a mechanical act or motion, then it clearly is not connected to enjoyment. But if praise is what flows from a heart that rejoices in the love of God, it is not only natural but enjoyable to praise God. *Praise, like rejoicing, is not just something you do, but it is something you are. It wells up inside you from your heart and explodes in a life of praise to God.*

We must understand this, or we will never understand the biblical concept of praise. All the passages, Psalms and expressions of praise in the Bible are the natural result of hearts that are thrilled to know God. If we don't see this, then we are like the little child reciting, "God is great. God is good, and we thank Him for our food" and calling it praise. God doesn't need our praise. We need to praise Him. We can't help but praise Him. Our hearts demand it.

In the very tender introduction to the church at Philippi, Paul expressed deep personal and spiritual affection for the Christians (Philippians 1:1-11). He told them about his prayer that they grow in love (v. 9), have a pure heart (v. 10), and be filled with the fruit of righteousness (v. 11). All of this would be "to the glory and praise of God."

Growing in love, sincerity and righteousness is praising God. In other words, praise is a condition of the heart. Praise is more than singing; it is being full of God. When we assemble together, we have a chance to share our common joy over God's presence in our lives. In every other area of life, praise is associated with thanks, appreciations and, hence, joy. Why should the assembly be any different? To talk about coming together to praise God and not see it as enjoyable is a contradiction of terms. Praise is the expressing of joy.

We need to remember that praise, at least from a New Testament point of view, is not a matter of raising our faces toward heaven and saying, "Praise the Lord." God is praised because we live in obedience to His will. We live to the "praise of His glory" (Ephesians 1:12), or as the Hebrew writer declared, "Let us continually offer up a sacrifice of praise to God" (Hebrews 13:15).

Closely related to praise, if not synonymous, is thanksgiving. I am not talking about a meal with turkey, but a feast on the fruit of the Spirit. A balanced diet of love, joy, peace, patience, kindness, goodness, faithfulness, gentleness and self-control will give anyone a different perspective on life (Galatians 5:22,23). For one thing, it will enable us to "in everything give thanks" (2 Thessalonians 5:18). In fact, it is "God's will" that we be thankful people. Again, this cannot be artificially manufactured. Giving thanks begins in the heart and can be consistently given only when a heart is full of love, joy, peace and the other fruit of the Spirit.

Have you ever considered how much of our assembly is dedicated to giving thanks? Thanksgiving is in every element of what we do: singing, praying, giving, preaching, communion and fellowship. Maybe I should rephrase that statement and say it "should be" in every element of our assembly. Sometimes we may have difficulty being thankful for the assembly itself let alone specific elements. Unfortunately our assemblies seem to avoid joy, and thanksgiving is a expression of joy.

As mentioned, joy and thanksgiving are matters of the heart and not the surrounding circumstances. James said that when we suffer hardships, we should "consider it all joy" because we know what it leads to (James 1:2). But, I don't believe James was referring to the assembly as one of those hardships. The assembly is to *cause* joy and thanksgiving instead of these things happening *in spite* of the assembly. Thanksgiving is one of the characteristics that distinguishes us as children of God. Listen to Paul:

> Therefore be imitators of God, as beloved children; and walk in love, just as Christ also loved you, and gave Himself up for us, an offering and a sacrifice to God as a fragrant aroma. But do not let immorality or any impurity or greed even be named among you, as is proper among the saints; and there must be no filthiness and silly talk, or coarse jesting, which are not fitting, but rather giving of thanks. (Ephesians 5:1-4)

Thanksgiving is one of the things that makes us different from the world. We give thanks as the result of our being enveloped by Christ's love. In Colossians 2:6,7, Paul described Christians and their relationship with Christ by using terms like "walk in Him," "rooted," "built up in Him," "established," and "overflowing with gratitude." "Overflowing" gratitude means that it can't be held back. Thanksgiving is a heart overflowing with the fruit of the Spirit such as love, joy and peace. That's why Paul could describe us as needing "an attitude of thanksgiving" (Colossians 4:2).

An old song declares that love and marriage naturally go together just like a horse and carriage. That is the way I would describe thanksgiving and joy. When you are thankful, you are joyful; when you are joyful, you are thankful. When Paul expressed his feelings for the brethren at Thessalonica he said, "For what thanks can we render to God for you in return for all the joy with which we rejoice before our God on your account" (1 Thessalonians 3:9).

We have so much to be thankful for when we assemble together that it is difficult to understand why we feel the need for our assembly to be such a solemn, sad occasion. Enjoy your faith. Enjoy grace and love. Enjoy the family of God. Let your assembly overflow with happiness, rejoicing, praise and thanksgiving. Let's turn our thumbs up and choose to live.

THUMBS UP FAITH

A while back, one of our teenagers at church was facing serious surgery. Tim is such a courageous young Christian that he has been an inspiration to the entire congregation. I never will forget the encouraging smile and thumbs up he gave as they rolled him away for his surgery. He inspired me to write a little song in his honor, and I later taught to to the congregation. The song is called "Thumbs Up Faith."

(Chorus)
I've got a thumbs up kind of faith in a thumbs down
   kind of world.
I've got a thumbs up kind of faith in a thumbs down
   kind of world.
With a lot of love from my God above to help
   me when I fall,
I've got a thumbs up kind of faith, and I'm feeling
   ten feet tall.

All week long I work with folks who give me no
   relief.
All week long I work with folks who only give me
   grief.
It's such a joy to be with Saints on Our Lord's
   special Day.

141

He gives me thumbs up kind of faith, and makes me
want to say, (Chorus)

Some will say that God is dead but I know that's
not true.
He sent His Son to live and die to save both me
and you.
He rules my life as Lord and King, and helps me
every day.
He gives me thumbs up kind of faith that makes me
sing and say, (Chorus)

Some day soon we'll be there before our Father's
throne,
And we'll all be wondering if we'll be going home.
He'll raise His hand and make a fist with thumb
pointing to the sky,
Because of thumbs up kind of faith we'll
be together by and by. (Chorus)

How do you turn your assembly into a thumbs up
experience? Determining how you are going to
accomplish the task is where the enjoyment begins.
The last thing you need is for me or anyone else to
outline what you need or to develop a new set of traditions. Key in on togetherness. Think people, not
performance. Enjoy the liberty that God has given you
to make your assembly the highlight of your week.

Many are going to have serious heartburn over the
idea that we assemble to increase our level of joy.
They will say, "It sounds so selfish and flippant." *We
need to understand that New Testament joy is not
synonymous with jubilation or a "tingly, happy feeling running up and down my spine." In fact, joy is*

serious business in the Bible. David's plea for forgiveness in Psalm 51:12 was "Restore to me the joy of Thy salvation." That joy can be present in pain, comfort in crisis, and warmth during life's cold spells. Far from being self-centered, joy is the result of being Christ-centered. After all, as Solomon wrote in Ecclesiastes 2:25, "Who can have enjoyment without Him?"

DISCUSSION QUESTIONS

1. Why is joy a very serious concept?

2. What do happiness, rejoicing, praising and thanksgiving have in common?

3. Why are churches fearful of emotionalism? Are happiness, rejoicing, praising and thanksgiving intellectual or emotional actions? Are they both?

4. Would you feel uncomfortable showing appreciation for someone in the assembly by applauding? Why or why not?

5. What are some specific ways that we can be more thankful in the assembly?

SECTION FIVE
EVANGELISM
AND THE ASSEMBLY

CHAPTER FOURTEEN
Go Get 'Em, Tiger

Everyone loves a sure thing. We enjoy knowing ahead of time that we will succeed, win, or be on top. This certainly can happen when you leave nothing to chance, fate or luck. (Actually we call it faith, but faith isn't supposed to be chancy.)

Some things in life are sure things. Death and taxes are the most obvious. But, what about knowing when that shoe lace is going to break? You know. It will happen when you are in a hurry. When will your car decide to die? That doesn't involve guess work because you know. Your car will fail to start when you are late for a very important meeting, or as in the movies, when the gang of crazed killers is about to catch up with you. We won't even discuss when you will find out that you're out of toilet paper.

Let me tell you about a sure thing for preachers. There's no guessing to it. I guarantee that it will get results every time. Preach about evangelism. If a preacher wants to produce guilt, cause responses, and grab even the most dedicated, then he should preach about evangelism. It will get results every time, every place, with any group of Christians. We can bet on it (figuratively speaking, of course). It doesn't matter how committed you are, how much work you've done, or how much you have sacrificed; you always could have done more evangelizing. No one can escape the double edged sword of guilt that is wielded by the capable communicators in the church. Evangelism is a topic that any preacher or teacher can "lather" on. The goal is saving souls; the need is more involvement; and the tone is urgency.

We have soul-winning workshops, evangelism seminars, and training courses galore. We need all these resources. The church is declining; members are reclining; and leaders are pining. More important, people are dying each day in a country with thousands upon thousands of churches, but they don't know Jesus. *We do need preaching about evangelism and evangelistic preaching, but we don't need it in the assembly.*

As Solomon said, "There is an appointed time for everything" (Ecclesiastes 3:1). Evangelism has a time and a place, and it isn't the assembly. *I am not saying that evangelism never has a place in the assembly. I am saying that the primary purpose of the assembly is not to evangelize, but to build up, unify and strengthen one another through being together.* To word it differently, the assembly – if it accomplishes its goals – should cause evangelism, but it doesn't exist for evangelism.

In his insightful book *Sharpening the Focus of the Church*, Gene Getz makes this observation:

> But what about the church as an evangelistic center? First of all, let it be reemphasized strongly that one of the basic objectives of the church is to reach the unsaved world. But let it also be emphasized that the purpose of the "church gathered," as described in the New Testament, is not evangelism – but edification. God never intended for the pastor's primary responsibility to be that of evangelism; that is, to preach to unsaved people who are brought to church by church members.[28]

To use the assembly as a primary tool for evangelism is to rob it of its power to strengthen and build up the body of Christ. When the aim is evangelism, the assembly then is not a feast but a fast as members are served leftovers week after week. Visitors don't need to be browbeaten with the gospel, and members don't need to have a baptism in guilt on a weekly basis. The assembly is a celebration of Sonship, not a recruiting drive. The call in the New Testament is for Christians to assemble. This doesn't mean visitors aren't welcomed. They are very welcome. They are welcomed to see Christians encourage, equip and enjoy each other. As a result, the visitors will know we are His disciples because we love one another (John 13:35). Visitors will be attracted by the closeness and love they see. This is especially true for those who are looking for a church home. They see the warm, happy atmosphere and recognize that relationships will be made quickly at a place like that.

The failure to grasp this principle causes frustration on the part of members and can lead to disaster for the congregation. In *Why Churches Die*, Hollis Green is emphatic about the place of evangelism.

> Evangelism was never intended to be carried on inside the church building.... Evangelism is something that must take place outside the four walls of the church where the sinners are. The church building may be a place for revival and a place where believers come to be nourished up in faith, taught the doctrines of the Word, and strengthened as believers. But, soul winning, for the most part, is done outside the church sanctuary. The church at worship is a meeting of those already won. The gathering is to instruct, to experience, so they may in turn become effective witnesses for Christ. Believers are to go forth into the community witnessing and winning those who are lost.[29]

The assembly is a catalyst for change, but the change is to take place in people who are already Christians, which is why I am dealing with this point. If we are going to be true to God's plan for us, we must use the assembly as the tool for which it was intended. If we don't use the assembly as God planned, then not only will we suffer spiritually, but we also will have less evangelism. You see, God's plan is that we "take the gospel," our plan is to say, "Come and get it." Whose plan will work best?

COME AND GO

The Great Commission is probably only second to John 3:16 in terms of popular knowledge. Most church folks know it by heart even if they don't know where to find it in the Bible. Jesus said:

> Go therefore and make disciples of all nations, baptiz-
> ing them in the name of the Father and the Son and
> the Holy Spirit, teaching them to observe all that I
> commanded you; and lo, I am with you always, even
> to the end of the age. (Matthew 28:19,20)

When it comes to spreading the Word of God and
making disciples, we must go forth and make it
happen. Our mission field is in our homes, neighbor-
hoods, schools, offices, and wherever people will
listen. The gospel is to be taken, delivered, offered
and shared.

Ironically although the Lord has told us to "go," we
have structured our evangelism around "come."
"Come to our nice facilities with comfortable seating,
regulated room temperature and traditional surroundings, and let our hired staff explain everything to you,"
we invite. We define evangelism as bringing someone
to church, inviting someone to the annual gospel
meeting, or being fortunate enough to have a visitor
wander into the assembly.

Not only is this view of evangelism unproductive
and unbiblical, but it also puts the congregation into a
position of being too comfortable to even consider
doing anything beyond just attending church. Phillip
Keller says we have become a "community of emotional cripples" because we are too comfortable and
cozy to reach out to a needy world. He writes:

> Christ challenges us to go out and face the fury of the
> storm. He bids us climb the cliff and search the moun-
> tainside for the lost and straying. He compels us with
> His own compassion to accompany Him along the

151

highways and hedge rows in search of stragglers and self-willed sinners.[30]

If the assembly were used to accomplish what it was intended to accomplish, evangelism would be a natural result. Christians would be encouraged and have the strength to share the most important person in their life, Jesus. They would be equipped to handle the questions, the setbacks, the disappointments, the challenges and the opportunities. Their lives would be filled with a joy so special that those around them would be dying to know their secret. People who have been loved in the assembly are far more likely to share that love with a neighbor.

As you read through the book of Acts and examine the conversion stories, two patterns become obvious. In each case someone "went." (Even though Cornelius came to Peter, Peter was sent to Joppa to meet him.) The apostles, Philip and Ananias, all followed Jesus's command to "Go," and people became disciples.

Another common element in each conversion example is a personal touch. They practiced one-on-one evangelism, which is the most productive way to make disciples. It makes much better sense to have everyone involved than to expect the preacher to perform miracles. The days of tongues of fire, violent rushing wind, and speaking with other tongues (i.e., Pentecost, Acts 2) are long past.

WALK THE AISLE

If you need proof that many believe evangelism to

be an integral part of the assembly, just look at our attachment to having an invitation song. Where in the Bible do you read about an invitation song? If ever there was a traditional practice that became law, this is it. Some people actually tell their children that in order to become Christians they have to take that long walk down the aisle, in front of everyone, and make "the good confession" before the entire church. "It will make them more committed," the parents say. We have created a religious ritual without biblical authority, and we further institutionalize the assembly as the center of our faith.

"What if we don't have an invitation song, but someone wants to become a Christian?" someone cries. How did they ever get by in the New Testament without an invitation song? What has happened to the personal touch? One on one? Are we so unapproachable that someone has to publicly respond before that person can be helped in obeying Christ?

I have presented lessons about the role of women in the church and closed with an invitation song. What would a person be responding to in this type of lesson? What about the invitation song that follows a sermon on adultery? Such a sermon hardly will make one want to be baptized.

The point is simple: The assembly is a "one another" event, not a "win another" event. The emphasis is on togetherness, not evangelism. If the assembly is effective, evangelism will happen as a result of all the encouragement, equipping and enjoyment that takes place.

NURTURE AND STIMULATE

Joe Ellis, one of the church growth specialists of today, in his book *The Church On Target*, describes what takes place in the assembly as nurturing. He says nurturing and evangelism depend on each other, but they are very different as to when and where they take place. "Nurturing is an internal process to the church," he states. "Evangelism is an external one. Nurture deals with the quality of the Christian's life and the quality of life among Christians; evangelism is the impact of the individuals and the corporate church on the world outside."[31] The relationship between the two is a simple cause and effect situation. Nurturing will cause evangelism, which will increase the number of those needing nurturing.

The Hebrew writer clearly describes what is to happen when Christians get together: "Stimulate one another to love and good deeds" (10:24). Is this verse not referring to what happens as a result of the assembly? The real key to evangelism is teaching Christians what love is all about. The crowning objective or mission of every Christian is not evangelism, although some strongly believe it is. Some teach that evangelism is what we live and breathe for and that it is the only real fruit we can bear. That understanding is wrong. Our mission is to love. We have been called by God, His Son, and His inspired writers to love God with all our heart, mind, soul and strength and to love our neighbor as ourselves (Mark 12:30,31). This idea is taught obviously and consistently throughout the Bible. When we learn what love really is, evangelism will take care of itself. To evangelize without love "profits me nothing" (1 Corinthians 13:3). The assembly should be teaching people how to love and

154

making them feel loved. The assembly helps us stay committed to our mission.

In the dark cloud of the Vietnam War is a silver lining that sparkles with the courage and loyalty of the men and women who served there. The long black marble wall in Washington, D.C., speaks of soldiers who gave the ultimate sacrifice for their country. Some of those men died with the words "Charlie Mike" on their lips. Charlie Mike stands for "C" and "M", an acronym for "Continue the Mission." When men went out on dangerous assignments, the words that were never far from their lips were Charlie Mike. Many a leader, mortally wounded, encouraged his men with Charlie Mike, continue the mission.

Nineteen hundred years earlier, another leader hung on a cross, suspended between heaven and earth, and called on us to Charlie Mike – continue the mission. Love God. Love our neighbor. Love one another. As a result, the world will know that we belong to Him.

DISCUSSION QUESTIONS

1. Why should the assembly not be oriented toward evangelism?

2. Would you characterize your congregation's outreach program as primarily "come and see us" or "go get 'em"?

3. Can the assembly be used to equip Christians to evangelize? How?

4. How did people respond to the gospel in New Testament times when they didn't have an invitation song?

5. Why is love the key to evangelism?

SUMMARY

CHAPTER FIFTEEN
The 3-H Club

James A. Michener is one of the most widely read novelists of our day. Most of us have read at least one of his epics or seen a movie that was made from one of his books. One of his latest novels is *Poland*, another sweeping story which covers several generations and includes an enormous amount of history. At the close of *Poland*, a character named Barski, a Catholic bishop, recounts an experience he had while a prisoner at Auschwitz during World War II.

The Nazis at Auschwitz were particularly ruthless toward the priests and rabbis. They took special pleasure in demeaning all religious leaders and their religions because, in some twisted way, they thought that exalted their own religion.

One of the more horrifying ordeals that the priests and rabbis were forced to endure involved their being crowded into a tiny cell. The cell had only one small window, which was high above their heads. At dusk the Nazis would cram 60 or more of them into the little room fully expecting to find over half of them dead in the morning from suffocation. Barski was one of 19 who survived the first time he was jammed into the cell. He endured it twice and declared that no one could survive the terrifying ordeal three times.

The reason he survived that first time was because a Jewish rabbi whispered to him just before he entered the room, "Stand opposite the window." Barski was dumbfounded at first, but he soon discovered how sound the advice was. As soon as the door to the cell was shut, there was a mass scramble for position. The big and strong men fought their way to the window, while he wiggled his way to the opposite wall.

The air soon became scarce. Men struggled to intercept what little came into the window, and soon they were killing one another. Some were strangled; others were crushed to death, and others simply fainted and fell to the floor only to be stomped to oblivion. What saved Barski were the little snatches of air that drifted in over everyone's head to where he stood opposite the window. He was saved by the advice of the Jewish rabbi.

The next morning, when Barski realized that he'd lived through the ordeal, he began looking for the rabbi who'd saved him. Evidently, the man hadn't been put into the cell with them the night before because he wasn't part of the living or the dead, who were piled high on the floor.

The next day Barski saw the rabbi on the work

detail lifting huge rocks after he'd had no food or sleep. When the rabbi saw that Barski had survived, his eyes lit up and he made a move to go over and speak to Barski. But the moment he moved toward Barski, the guards knocked the rabbi to the ground and kicked him to death. Right before Barski's eyes, they kicked the man to death.

"As he lay there in the prison yard looking up at me," said Barski, "his face torn apart and covered with blood, I wanted with all the force in my body to rush over and comfort him, to take him in my arms, for he had saved my life and he deserved that consolation in the moments when he was leaving his. But I could not. I had no physical or moral power. The cell had been too terrible, and I stood motionless as they kicked my savior to death.

"What was the last thing he did on this earth? He smiled at me. Through the blood that dimmed his eyes he smiled at me, as if to say: 'Be not afraid.' I seemed to hear this little Jewish rabbi using the words of Jesus Christ."[32]

In the midst of the most horrifying experience of his life, this fictitious bishop learned the meaning of real love and real courage. It reminds me of another man who was carrying out a routine bit of cruelty, but it became anything but routine when the midday sun turned to darkness and the earth shook. As he watched the man on the cross breathe his last, the centurion said, "Truly this man was the Son of God" (Mark 15:39).

As we vicariously become a spectator at Golgotha, do our hearts ache with pain as our Savior is put to death? Have we truly grappled with the intense love and courage displayed by the one spread-eagled on that wooden crosspiece? Are we moved, compelled and committed? As we stand in the shadow of that ghastly spectacle, do we have the courage to re-evaluate our priorities? Do pet peeves slip back into their appropriate gutter, and do selfish whims wilt and die? Are we willing to think of all else as manure in order to know the surpassing value of having Jesus as Lord?

Nothing brings things into perspective as crisis does. Maybe that is why our focus is supposed to be "Christ and Him crucified." The crucifixion of Jesus is a crisis that we can use daily to jar us back into what really counts. The cross is a constant reminder of His sacrifice and our salvation. The cross reminds us that in all things our desire must be to please Him.

Many of the things discussed in this book are things that we talk about using words like "I believe," "I think," or "I prefer." It is easy to lose sight of our ultimate responsibility, which is pleasing Him, as we quibble about preferences, opinions, and even interpretations. We are here to walk with Him, but sometimes we walk all over Him as we cling to "our way of doing things." Just as a blood-spattered rabbi dying in Auschwitz could have all his differences with the other man enveloped and hidden by love, so we too can submerge our differences in the love that flowed from the cross of Calvary.

Those who read this book will cover the full spectrum of reactions. Some will see it as "old hat"; others will see it as radical; others will see it as heretical. The differences in reactions may depend on whether the reader's loyalty is to Jesus or to the traditions of man that have become law. *May God free us all from the fear of asking questions like "Why?", "How come?", and "Who says?" God is certainly not afraid of these*

162

kinds of questions. Why should we be?

This book is easy to summarize. Christians assemble because they need to be together. The elements of their togetherness should include encouraging, equipping and enjoying, things that cause evangelizing. When these things happen, God is glorified because of our obedience to His directions.

The summary in the preceding paragraph is simply stated, but it is complex and disturbing to some who believe corporate worship is being undermined. I want to offer three general suggestions as I conclude this study. These suggestions are offered as further explanation of what has been presented and as principles about which even the most "shocked" can agree.

HOLY

Above all else, the assembly must be holy. Even in areas of opinion where flexibility and freedom reign supreme, holiness must be the final coat of paint that covers the entire canvas. Why? Because Christians are called to be holy. We are a separate – set apart for a purpose – people. We have been called with a holy calling by a holy God, and we were told to be holy in both body and spirit (2 Timothy 1:9; John 17:11; 1 Corinthians 7:34).

Holiness is a way of life. Holiness is not an atmosphere in the sanctuary; it is an attitude in the heart. We run into difficulty again with this concept. To many, holiness is an aura, an ambiance, or a sense of the mysterious in the temple of God. Some believe that holiness is spiritual energy that is directed solely toward God who soaks up our praise and glories in

163

our solemnity; it is temple worship. These folks think that by saying that the assembly is for togetherness, it means having merely horizontal worship. They say that God has been left out.

I must admit: Temple worship is vertical worship. The problem is finding vertical worship in the New Testament. What is vertical worship? Is praising God a one way connection between the worshipper and Him? Is baptism a horizontal or a vertical act? When we sing and admonish one another with songs, hymns and spiritual songs, are we being merely horizontal? Is the contribution a horizontal act since the plate only goes sideways? What makes the sermon, the public prayers and the communion vertical?

The absolute primary responsibility of every child of God is to love Him with all our heart, soul, mind and strength and to love our neighbor as ourselves. Did God reduce that responsibility to being merely horizontal when He told John that the way to love God is to love one another? One-another love is the proof that God abides in us, that His love is perfected in us, and that we abide in Him. In fact, it is impossible to love God without loving our brothers. That sounds suspiciously horizontal.

Let's examine a simple question. Can anything holy be merely horizontal? In simple terms, it is not the direction of the act that counts, but rather the condition of the heart. Anything that God tells us to do is holy. Every time we are obedient to God, He is glorified. That is what praise is. It is not some act of homage or veneration. Praise is a life of obedience, sacrifice, and love. Paul said that we live to the praise of His glory (Ephesians 1:12). When we give a cup of cold water in His name, He is praised. When we lead a sinner to Jesus, all the host of heaven rejoices. When Christians get together and build one another up, and when their lives are more Christlike, He is praised. When we keep His commandments, He is praised. "And the one who keeps His commandments abides in Him, and He in him. And we know by this that He abides in us, by the Spirit which He has given us" (1 John 3:24). And isn't that what worship is all about?

When we say the assembly must be holy, it means we must be loyal to the Word. The Word must be treated as sacred and pure. We must have a rock-bed foundation that can come only from a total commitment to the truth. We never allow the precepts of men and their corresponding traditions to be elevated to the level of law. It means that we want only to do God's will and to be as obedient to Him as possible.

Another aspect of holiness in the assembly is an emphasis on the spiritual. That means we desire to be Christ-centered, soul stirring, life changing and heavenward bound. We need to be careful when we start creating a hierarchy of spiritual things (i.e. singing must be more spiritual than a fellowship dinner), but we must never lose sight of our eternal orientation. Encouragement, equipping and enjoyment must be seen as instruments of spiritual growth.

We always must remember, that holiness in the assembly means we are far more concerned with internal things than external acts. Holiness begins and ends in the heart. Brand-name clothes and silk ties never made anyone a better child of God. Perfect attendance never guaranteed anyone an E-ride through the gate of pearl. A church title never replaced transformation into the spirit of Christ. After centuries of reading about Zaccheus, centurions and the adulter-

165

ess, all of whom we would have pre-judged, pre-condemned and pre-written up, we continue to look at externals and completely ignore the condition of the heart. If it is indeed our desire to be like Jesus, we must imitate His ability to see beyond the externals.

HELPFUL

He lived in a graveyard. The white coat brigade had tried to restrain him with chains and shackles. He simply ripped the chains and shackles apart and overpowered anyone who tried to hold him. His piercing screams echoed through the hills as his tormented mind caused him to bash himself with stones. His body was covered with gashes, bruises and scrapes.

The arrival of Jesus was enough to bring the wild man down from the graveyard. The screaming madman fell at the feet of Jesus, slobbering, jerking uncontrollably, and looking more dead than alive. The army of unclean spirits that possessed him were driven out at the command of Jesus. They entered into a herd of 2,000 swine, who at once rushed off a cliff into the sea.

The man was healed. He was normal again. Soon he sat at Jesus's feet, clean, clothed and completely sane. The inner peace was written on his face. The gratitude was in his eyes and on his heart. Jesus had helped him, and he never would forget the debt he owed. When the time came for Jesus to leave, the former tomb tenant begged to accompany Him. Jesus told him to "Go home to your people and report to them what great things the Lord has done for you" (Mark 5:1-20). He had been helped and now it was his turn

166

to be the helper.

Can a gathering of Christlike people be anything less than helpful? With the need we all have to grow in grace and knowledge, we must be concerned about helping each other. We can help each other, in a variety of ways, but we should all be able to agree that the assembly should be helpful. After all, if the assembly is not helpful, what is it?

Was it not God's intent that those things we do when we assemble help us? This idea is important to understand. The things that Christians do together in the assembly are not rituals. They are tools – tools to help us grow, change, fine tune or dismantle. They were meant to be used, not performed.

The Lord's Supper is a tool to tighten our fellowship and realign our sights on the cross. Giving is a tool that keeps us in tune with God, the author of giving. It helps us run cheerfully and productively. Prayer is the tool we use to keep in touch with the master Mechanic who can fix any problem and make all things work together for good. Singing is the sound of a precision machine. It sounds so beautiful that you ignore the few dings, dents, and scratches on the outside. And preaching is the constant sharing of the owner's manual, an irreplaceable tool to any smooth running machine.

Being helpful in the assembly means that needs are being met. People who are hurt need healing. People in pain need comforting. Those searching for direction need guidance. Folks down in the dumps need uplifting. Jesus always met needs. His church should, too. *When we decide we are meeting together to help each other and not to perform rituals, people will begin to see what God has always wanted them to see – love in action.* This may mean that we drop back and review what an "expediency" is and in what areas we have the freedom to do what is expedient. Once we are sure we are following God's direction, the question then becomes "What is best for us?" rather than "What does everybody else do?" How can we best meet needs? What is the best way to use our facilities? What is the best time for assemblies? What is the best format for our assemblies? What is the best way to do God's will? Let's make sure we have biblical authority and freedom, and then let's proceed with what works best.

How many times have we assembled together and studied the story of the Good Samaritan? After these lessons we have marched out the door, passing folks who've been beaten and left by the roadside. We pass by them in the foyer of the church building: People whose marriages are falling apart; families torn by drugs, alcohol, suicide, death, divorce and unemployment; and persons with a hundred other social ills, and we don't have time to deal with hurt; we have to go home and get ready for the next church service. The priest and Levite are not as sinister as we might think. After all, they were church leaders.

What if we were to get so busy helping folks we never had time to attend church? Heresy! One of the most bone-chilling passages of Scripture in the New Testament speaks to this point; it is Jesus' description of Judgment in Matthew 25. What a shock to hear that God never asked about church attendance. He never showed any interest in Bible School Perfect Attendance Certificates. He did not check the total of contribution given or souls saved. What is the chief concern at Judgment? How much loving help did you give? How many needy folks did you reach out to? The hungry, the thirsty, the stranger, the naked, the sick and the imprisoned asked for help. Did you give it?

The assembly should be help, give help and cause help. "Let us therefore draw near with confidence to the throne of grace, that we may receive mercy and may find grace to help in time of need" (Hebrews 4:16).

HEAVENLY

At the publication of this book, I have spent fifteen wonderful years of ministry with two loving congregations. During that time scores of loved ones have been transferred away or transported to Abraham's bosom. Whether the event was a farewell fellowship or a funeral, the pain of separation cut deeply into my heart. So I have announced to all our folks that when they get to the gate of heaven, we will all get together on the right side of the gate until everyone is there. Then we will all enter together. What a great reunion that will be!

While the comment is somewhat tongue-in-cheek, the thought of a heavenly homecoming takes much of the bite out of goodbye. We are all flesh and blood and we meet in a building of brick and mortar, but our goal is to be part of an eternal congregation that never will see death, pain or tears again. The assembly should keep heaven before our eyes.

The assembly reminds us of heaven, but it also prepares us for heaven by helping us to grow spiritually and by giving us a taste of what it will be like. *The warm sense of love that pervades our togetherness and the joy of salvation combine to give us an appe-tizer to the main course of heaven*. The Hebrew writer described Christians as having "tasted of the heavenly gift" (Hebrews 6:4). Every time we meet together we're reminded of our desire to be together, for eternity with Jesus in heaven. We can taste how great it will be. We feel now those things that will be enhanced by heaven – things like love, peace, joy, and Jesus.

CONCLUSION

Deep in grief the two men walked the road to Emmaus. The man from Nazareth had been entombed for three days, and now no one knew where the body was. All the hopes and grand ideas of the two men were empty, like the tomb. Along the way they picked up a third traveler, which gave them a reason to rehash their despair one more time.

When the trio stopped for supper, they plopped down at the table, worn out emotionally as much as physically. When the third man, the stranger, picked up the bread, something about his mannerisms caught their attention. Then he blessed the bread and broke it, giving them each a section.

Like the lighting of an oil lamp, recognition lit up

their eyes. Before them sat Jesus the Nazarene, risen from the dead. Then He disappeared like a puff of smoke. When the shock of what they'd seen wore off, one of the men whispered, "Were not our hearts burning within us while He was speaking to us on the road, while He was explaining the Scriptures to us?" They jumped up at once and raced to Jerusalem. They had a story to tell (Luke 24:13-35).

When Jesus is present, hearts are affected. A heartless assembly is a Christless assembly. He must be the object of our get-togethers. The time has come for hearts to start burning in the assembly. Genuine *koinonia* must not be relegated to "something less official than the worship hour." It is worship. Jesus is crying to be heard, and hearts are desperately needing to burn with His message of love, care and hope. Ritualism, traditionalism and formalism have given us a plastic religion in place of the pure crystal of shared lives and Christlike spirits. *The future must hold the promise of deeper relationships with brethren, more opportunities to give loving help, and a relevant assembly that encourages, equips, builds joy and saves souls.*

The past is unchangeable. Damage has been done because we blindly followed traditions and generally forgot the reason why we assemble. We can't undo the past, but we can improve the future. The future is charged with possibilities and potential. We must choose to attack it with faith, battle it with love, and save it by grace. But the past, well, to slightly alter an old proverb – there is no sense crying over spilt grape juice.

DISCUSSION QUESTIONS

1. What elements of your assembly fit into the category of expediencies?

2. In what ways must the assembly be holy?

3. Is an action that is done in obedience to God merely a horizontal or man-centered act?

4. If an assembly is needs oriented, does that mean it is not God-centered?

5. When something is in the realm of an expediency, is it inappropriate to say, "Let's do what is best for us"?

6. Is your assembly structured to discover needs and help heal hurts? What would need to change for that to happen?

7. If the assembly is a taste of heaven, would the prospects of spending eternity in the assembly be an exciting idea to you?

8. What would you change about your assembly to make it a little more like "heaven on earth"?

ENDNOTES

1. Joseph Henry Thayer, *Greek-English Lexicon of the New Testament* (New York: American Book Corp., 1886) p. 548.
2. William F. Arndt and F. Wilbur Gingrich, *A Greek-English Lexicon of the New Testament and Other Early Christian Literature* (Grand Rapids, MI: Zondervan Publishing House, 1957) p. 723.
3. Thayer, p. 372.
4. Robert Cushman, "Worship as Acknowledgment," *Worship in Scripture and Tradition* (New York: Oxford University Press, 1963) p. 33.
5. William Barclay, *The Letter to the Romans* (Philadelphia: The Westminister Press, 1955) p. 168.
6. V.L. Stanfield, *The Christian Worshipping* (Nashville: Convention Press, 1965) p. 17.
7. *Real Worship*, quoted in William Temple, *Readings in St. John's Gospel*, First Series (London: Macmillan and Co., 1939) p. 68.
8. Warren Wiersbe, *Real Worship* (Nashville: Oliver Nelson, 1986) p. 27.
9. Gerhard Dilling, *Worship in the New Testament* (Philadelphia: The Westminister Press, 1962) p. 21.
10. Graham Kendrick, *Learning to Worship As a Way of Life* (Minneapolis: Bethany House Publishers, 1984) p. 24.
11. Gene A. Getz, *Sharpening the Focus of the Church* (Chicago: Moody Press, 1974) pp. 200-201.
12. John MacArthur, Jr., *The Ultimate Priority* (Chicago: Moody Press, 1983) p. 13.
13. MacArthur, p. 22.
14. Everett Ferguson, *Early Christians Speak* (Austin, TX: Sweet Publishing Company, 1971) p. 75.
15. Jerry and Mary White, *Friends and Friendships* (Colorado Springs: Navpress, 1982) p. 144.
16. Ferguson, p. 76.
17. Mosie Lister, "Where No One Stands Alone," in *Songs of the Church*, ed. by Alton T. Howard (West Monroe, LA: Harvard Pub. Co., 1977) p. 537.
18. Kendrick, pp. 204-205.
19. Kenneth Blanchard and Spencer Johnson, *The One Minute Manager* (New York: William Morrow and Comp., Inc., 1982) p. 101.

20. W.E. Vine, *Expository Dictionary of New Testament Words* Vol. II E-Li. (Old Tappan, NJ: Revell Company, 1966 edition) p. 26.

21. Kendrick, p. 11.

22. Andy T. Richie, Jr., *Thou Shalt Love the Lord Thy God* (Austin, TX: Firm Foundation Publishing House, 1969) p. 7.

23. Michael Barthorp, *The Zulu War* (Poole, Dorset: Blandford Press, 1980) pp. 45-70.

24. Kendrick, p. 11.

25. William L. Coleman, *The Pharisee's Guide to Total Holiness* (Minneapolis: Bethany House Publishers, 1977) p. 40.

26. Donald L. Babner and Sarah Ricketts, *Building People Through a Caring Sharing Fellowship* (Wheaton, IL: Tyndale House Publisher, Inc., 1978) p. 43.

27. Vine, pp. 270-271.

28. Getz, p. 205.

29. Hollis L. Green, *Why Churches Die* (Minneapolis: Bethany Fellowship, 1972) p. 45.

30. W. Phillip Keller, *Walking With God* (Old Tappan, NJ: Fleming H. Revell Company, 1989) p. 25.

31. Joe E. Ellis, *The Church on Target* (Cincinnati: Standard Publishing, 1986) p. 19.

32. James A. Michener, *Poland* (New York: Random House, 1983) pp. 547-548.

BIBLIOGRAPHY

Arndt, William F., and Gingrich, F. Wilbur. *A Greek Lexicon of the New Testament*. Grand Rapids, MI: Zondervan Publishing House, 1957.

Babner, Donald L., and Ricketts, Sarah. *Building People Through a Caring, Sharing Fellowship*. Wheaton, IL: Tyndale House Publisher, Inc., 1978.

Barclay, William. *The Letter to the Romans*. Philadelphia: The Westminister Press, 1955.

Barthrop, Michael. *The Zulu War*. Poole, Dorset: Blandford Press, 1980.

Blanchard, Kenneth, and Spencer, Johnson. *The One Minute Manager*. New York: William Morrow and Company, Inc., 1982.

Coleman, William L. *The Pharisee's Guide to Total Holiness*. Minneapolis: Bethany House Publishers, 1977.

Cushman, Robert. "Worship as Acknowledgment," *Worship in Scripture and Tradition*. New York: Oxford University Press, 1963.

Dilling, Gerhard. *Worship in the New Testament*. Philadelphia: The Westminister Press, 1962.

Ellis, Joe E. *The Church on Target*. Cincinnati: Standard Publishing, 1986.

Ferguson, Everett. *Early Christians Speak*. Austin, TX: Sweet Publishing Company, 1971.

Getz, Gene A. *Sharpening the Focus of the Church*. Chicago: Moody Press, 1974.

Green, Hollis L. *Why Churches Die*. Minneapolis: Bethany Fellowship, 1972.

Keller, W. Phillips. *Walking With God*. Old Tappan, NJ: Fleming H. Revell , 1989.

Kendrick, Graham. *Learning to Worship as a Way of Life*. Minneapolis: Bethany House Publishers, 1984.

Lister, Mosie. "Where No One Stands Alone." *In Songs of the Church*, p. 537. Edited by Alton H. Howard. West Monroe, LA: Harvard Pub. Co., 1977.

MacArthur, John Jr. *The Ultimate Priority*. Chicago: Moody Press, 1983.

Michener, James A. *Poland*. New York: Random House, 1983.

Real Worship. Quoted in William Temple, *Readings in St. John's Gospel*, p. 22. London: MacMillan and Co., 1939.

Richie, Andy T. Jr. *Thou Shalt Love the Lord Thy God*. Austin, TX: Firm Foundation Publishing House, 1969.

Stanfield, V.L. *The Christian Worshipping*. Nashville: Convention Press, 1965.

Thayer, Joseph Henry. *Greek-English Lexicon of the New Testament*. New York: American Book Corp., 1886.

Vine, W.E. *Expository Dictionary of New Testament Words*. Vol. II. Old Tappan, NJ: Revell , 1966 edition.

White, Jerry and Mary. *Friends and Friendships*. Colorado Springs: Navpress, 1982.

Wiersbe, Warren. *Real Worship*. Nashville: Oliver Nelson, 1986.